2-

W9-CJT-648

EXPLORERS *and* EXPLORATION

VOLUME 8

AFRICA AND ARABIA

Geoffrey Nowell-Smith

Grolier Educational

SHERMAN TURNPIKE, DANBURY, CONNECTICUT 06816

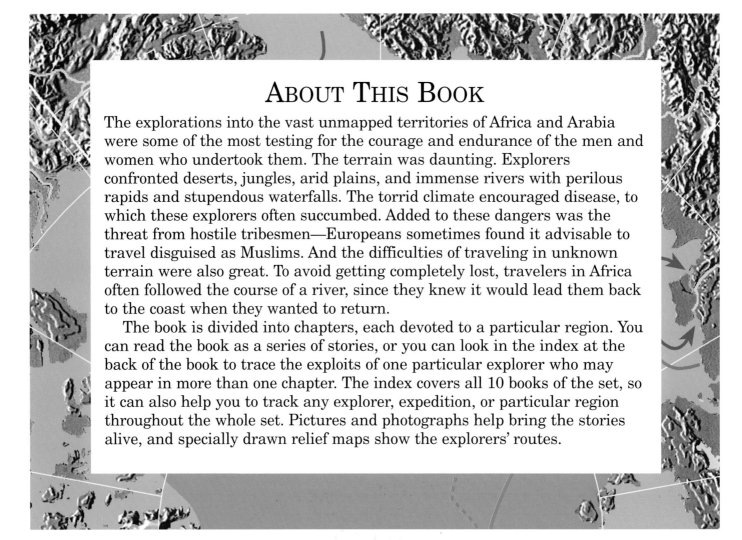

ABOUT THIS BOOK

The explorations into the vast unmapped territories of Africa and Arabia were some of the most testing for the courage and endurance of the men and women who undertook them. The terrain was daunting. Explorers confronted deserts, jungles, arid plains, and immense rivers with perilous rapids and stupendous waterfalls. The torrid climate encouraged disease, to which these explorers often succumbed. Added to these dangers was the threat from hostile tribesmen—Europeans sometimes found it advisable to travel disguised as Muslims. And the difficulties of traveling in unknown terrain were also great. To avoid getting completely lost, travelers in Africa often followed the course of a river, since they knew it would lead them back to the coast when they wanted to return.

The book is divided into chapters, each devoted to a particular region. You can read the book as a series of stories, or you can look in the index at the back of the book to trace the exploits of one particular explorer who may appear in more than one chapter. The index covers all 10 books of the set, so it can also help you to track any explorer, expedition, or particular region throughout the whole set. Pictures and photographs help bring the stories alive, and specially drawn relief maps show the explorers' routes.

Published 1998 by Grolier Educational
Sherman Turnpike
Danbury, Connecticut 06816

© 1998 Brown Partworks Ltd

Set ISBN: 0-7172-9135-9
Volume ISBN: 0-7172-9143-X

Cover picture: AKG, London

All rights reserved. Except for use in a review, no part of this book may be reproduced, stored in a retrieval system, or transmitted in any form, or by any means, electronic, mechanical photocopying, recording, or otherwise, without prior permission of Grolier Educational.

For information address the publisher:
Grolier Educational, Sherman Turnpike, Danbury, Connecticut 06816

Library of Congress Cataloging-in-Publication Data
Grolier student library of explorers and exploration
p.cm.—Includes indexes.—Contents: vol.1. The earliest explorers—vol.2. The golden age of exploration—vol.3. Europe's imperial adventurers—vol.4. Scientists and explorers—vol.5. Latin America—vol.6. North America—vol.7. Australasia and Asia—vol.8. Africa and Arabia—vol.9. Polar explorers—vol.10. Space and underwater.

1. Discoveries in geography—Juvenile literature. 2. Explorers—Juvenile literature. [1. Discoveries in geography. 2. Explorers.] I. Grolier Educational Corporation.
G175.G75 1997   97-27683
910.9—dc.21   CIP
                                                    AC

For Brown Partworks Ltd
Editor: Shona Grimbly
Designers: Joan Curtis and Paul Griffin
Picture Research: Jenny Silkstone
Maps: David Heidenstam
Text editor: Matt Turner

Printed in Singapore

CONTENTS

Africa and Arabia

SO. NORWALK BRANCH LIBRARY
10 Washington Street
Norwalk, CT 06854
Tel. 899-2790

Mary Evans Picture Library

EARLY EXPLORERS IN AFRICA

The 15th century saw a great surge in exploration. Until that time Africa had remained almost unknown to Europeans. In the Middle Ages Arab and Berber traders had made the trek across the vast Sahara Desert in search of gold and slaves, and Arab sailors had made their way down the east coast as far as the island of Zanzibar.

In the early 15th century the Portuguese started a series of expeditions and exploratory voyages that were to lead, three-quarters of a century later, to the discovery of a sea route around Africa to the Orient. But they kept close to the coast and coastal strips, and for a long time the forests and uplands of the interior of Africa remained unexplored.

Below: Madeira off the African coast. The first Portuguese expedition sent out by Henry the Navigator discovered the island group by accident after being blown off course.

Genevieve Leaper; Ecoscene/Corbis

The Portuguese explorations began in 1415 with a land expedition led by King John I to capture Ceuta, an Arab port on the south side of the Strait of Gibraltar.

PRINCE HENRY THE NAVIGATOR

The king left behind his son Henry to govern the town. The imagination of the young prince was fired by stories told about the trade routes deep into Africa and about a Christian kingdom, ruled by the legendary priest-king Prester John, that might exist in eastern Africa.

In 1418 Henry sent out the first of many seaborne expeditions that were to earn him the name Henry the Navigator. Led by João Gonçalves Zarco and Tristão Vaz Teixeira, this expedition was blown off course and ended up on the island of Porto Santo in the Madeiras off the African coast. The following year Henry was made governor of the province of the Algarve in Portugal and took up residence in Sagres, which was to be his headquarters for the rest of his life.

Throughout the 1420s Henry's seafarers worked their way down the African coast as far as Cape Bojador, directly

Below: Prince Henry the Navigator, son of King John I of Portugal. Henry founded a school of navigation and encouraged the development of improved navigational aids, such as the backstaff and quadrant.

Hulton Getty

Ibero-Amerikanischer Institut, Berlin/AKG, London

Left: Prince Henry consults sea charts with his squires. These young men made up for their scant experience in exploration with their bravery and taste for adventure. This was just as well because Africa in the 15th century had plenty of horrors in store for experts and novices alike.

south of the Canary Islands. These expeditions were primitive affairs conducted in small but sturdy square-rigged vessels designed for coastal trade.

THE CARAVEL

For ocean-going voyages, Henry reasoned, larger vessels would be needed, capable of withstanding gale-force winds but light and maneuverable at the same time. A new type of ship was commissioned—the caravel—that is first mentioned in a report of 1441. A prototype caravel was almost certainly used as early as 1434 when the young Gil Eannes managed to round the dangerous reefs off Cape Bojador and push forward to the Tropic of Cancer at latitude 23° North.

Soon the explorers were meeting people who were not brown-skinned Berbers but black Africans from south of the

Darrell Gulin/Corbis

Sahara Desert. In 1441 the caravels brought back a handful of gold dust and a small group of Africans, who were sold as slaves. Further expeditions under Dinís Dias and Nuno Tristão reached the Senegal River (1445) and rounded Cape Verde, the westernmost point of Africa.

To lead his early expeditions Henry had appointed squires. They were country boys, chosen for their bravery and sense of adventure rather than for their experience or learning. One of these young men, João Fernandes, spent several months stranded near Capo Branco in 1444–1445 before being rescued. On his return he gave a lively and detailed report on the customs of the Berber and Azenegue people he encountered.

PRESTER JOHN'S KINGDOM

In 1428 Henry's elder brother Pedro had returned from a long journey across Europe, bringing back a copy of the *Travels* of Marco Polo as well as much important knowledge about the East. Henry became more and more convinced of the need to find Prester John's elusive kingdom, which Pedro thought was to be found in Abyssinia (Ethiopia). But Pedro was killed in 1449 by the supporters of Afonso, the new king of Portugal, and Henry's dream of finding the legendary kingdom was never to be realized.

CADAMOSTO HEADS INLAND

In 1454 Alvise da Cadamosto, a Venetian merchant, presented himself at Henry's court. He was interested in exploring Africa, but his motives were commercial—he wanted a share of any profits. He was an educated and observant man, and with his recruitment geographical discovery took a new turn. He reported on customs and systems of government among the Africans and on the adornment of their bodies.

Henry commissioned Cadamosto to explore the coast of Africa with a view to establishing trading connections with the local people. Henry supplied him with a ship and a crew, and Cadamosto set sail to the south in 1455.

In 1455 the Venetian merchant Alvise da Cadamosto traveled up the Gambia River in search of trading prospects. He brought back reports of the African wildlife he had encountered, which included elephants (below).

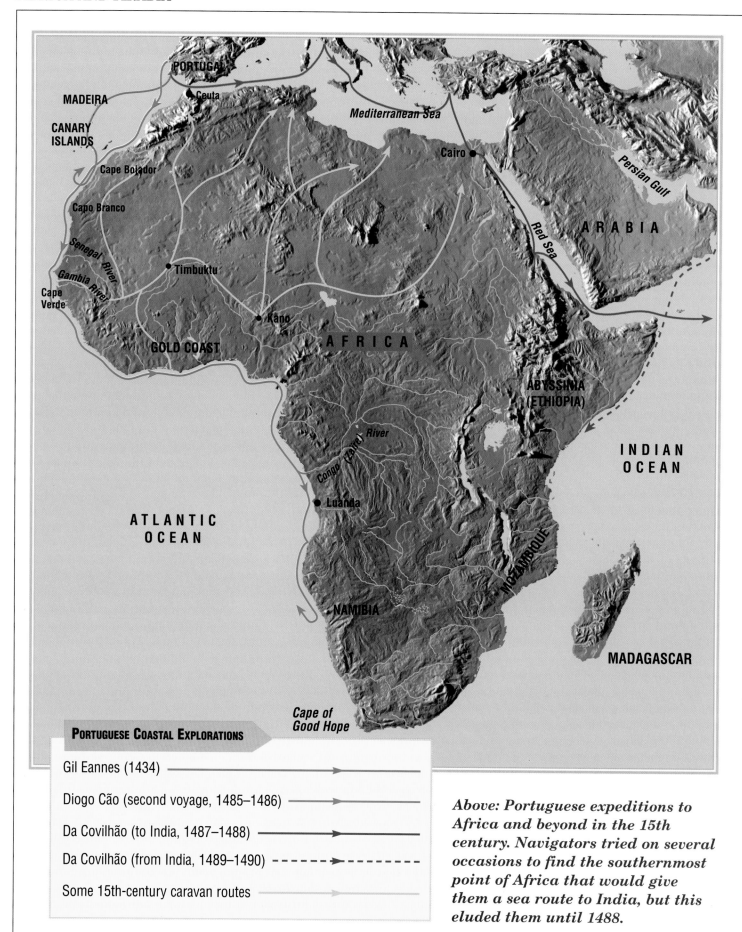

PORTUGUESE COASTAL EXPLORATIONS

Gil Eannes (1434) ——————————————→

Diogo Cão (second voyage, 1485–1486) ——————————→

Da Covilhão (to India, 1487–1488) ——————————→

Da Covilhão (from India, 1489–1490) - - - - - - →

Some 15th-century caravan routes ——————————→

Above: Portuguese expeditions to Africa and beyond in the 15th century. Navigators tried on several occasions to find the southernmost point of Africa that would give them a sea route to India, but this eluded them until 1488.

An Ecological Disaster

In 1418, on their very first expedition down the African coast, Prince Henry's sailors were blown off course and took refuge on a small island that they called Porto Santo. Returning in force two years later, the sailors, led by João Gonçalves Zarco and Tristão Vaz Teixeira, discovered another larger island just beyond it, which they named Madeira. The senior captains divided Madeira between themselves, leaving Porto Santo to a third member of the party, Bartolomeu Perestrello.

Perestrello had with him a pregnant doe rabbit that gave birth during the voyage. Mother and babies were let loose on the island. With no predators to limit their number, the rabbits multiplied. This was the first known case of a kind of ecological disaster that has happened many times since. All the crops planted by the colonists were eaten, and it took many years— and a ruthless campaign of extermination—to reestablish the island's ecology.

Below: Porto Santo in the Madeiras, where Portuguese sailors let rabbits loose—with disastrous results—in the early 1400s.

Not content with coastal exploration, Cadamosto explored the Senegal River, reaching 60 miles (100 km) inland and being entertained as a guest for a month by the local ruler. He then carried on to the Gambia River, which he traveled up for 11 days, recording descriptions of elephants, hippopotamuses, crocodiles, and other wildlife. However, during this expedition he was attacked by local tribesmen in canoes and had to make a hasty retreat to the open sea.

A monopoly on West Africa

After Henry's death in 1460 the pace of exploration slackened. Then in 1469 King Afonso, who had no interest in exploration, farmed out the enterprise to a merchant called Fernão Gomes. Gomes's contract gave him a monopoly on the West African trade, provided his ships explored 100 leagues (about 300 miles/480 km) of new coast a year.

Jonathan Blair/Corbis

By 1475 Gomes had explored right around the bulge in the coast of West Africa. In six years he had achieved as much as Henry the Navigator's explorers had achieved in 30 years.

IN FOR A SHOCK

The Portuguese were now close to the Equator, heading east, and it seemed they would soon be around the toe of Africa and could strike for the Indies.

But they were in for a shock. A few hundred miles on the coastline turned south again, and it was clear that the African landmass stretched an indefinite distance to the south. Undaunted, they persevered.

PORTUGUESE NAVIGATION

In making their calculations, the Portuguese made good use of the latest astronomical and mapmaking techniques. The traditional world map in the

Middle Ages was the *mappa mundi*; it showed the world as a flat disc with Jerusalem at the center. This was, of course, quite useless for navigation. So in the 15th century Catalan and Italian sailors developed a new type of map, the portolan chart. This showed ports and other geographical features connected by lines showing distances and directions.

To calculate latitude, the Portuguese used the quadrant, an instrument held to the eye to measure the height of the sun at midday. This was extremely accurate but could not be used in cloud or on the deck of a rocking ship.

Longitude was determined by a system called dead reckoning. The word dead is short for deduced, because the sailors deduced their position from an estimate of how far they had traveled and in what direction. Dead reckoning was prone to errors, but these could be corrected by repeated observation, and it

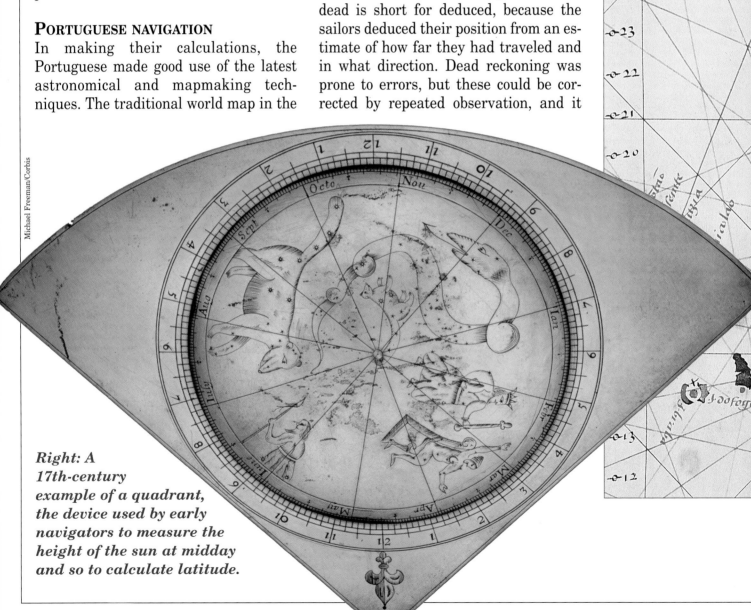

Michael Freeman/Corbis

Right: A 17th-century example of a quadrant, the device used by early navigators to measure the height of the sun at midday and so to calculate latitude.

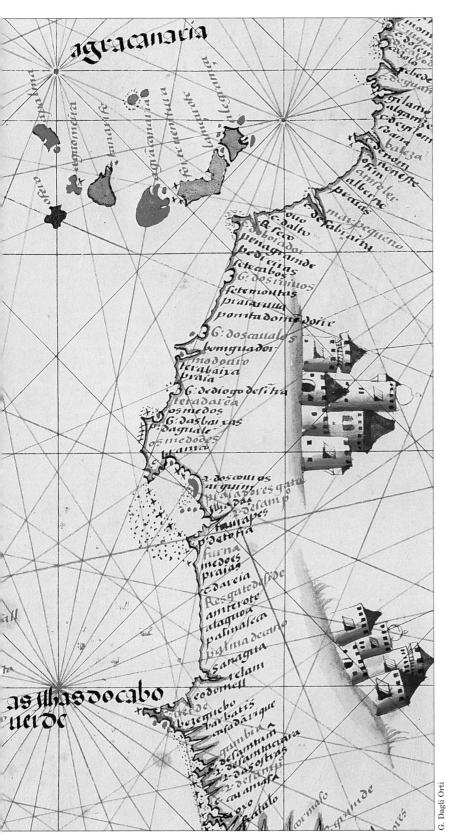

Above: A Portuguese map of 1514 showing the West African coast at Cape Verde. This was as far as Prince Henry's young sailors had been able to reach.

did not take the Portuguese long to chart not only the African coast but also the many islands they found offshore.

JOHN II TAKES OVER
In 1481 Afonso was succeeded as king by John II. John was determined to follow in Henry's footsteps. He assembled a new team of expert advisers and prepared for the final prize: the discovery of where Africa really ended. Then the route to the Indies would truly be open.

A sailor had brought back more rumors of a Christian kingdom in Africa.

Diogo Cão was the leader of the next voyages. In 1482 he reached the mouth of the Congo (now Zaïre) River and pushed on south beyond Luanda to a point he named Cape of Santa Maria, marking the site with a stone cross.

Cão made a second voyage in 1485, sure that he would reach the southern tip of Africa. This was not to be. He got as far as Cape Cross, on the coast of what is now Namibia. It is thought that he may have died at sea, and the expedition returned without him.

Meanwhile King John was preparing his masterstroke. A sailor named João Afonso de Aveiro had brought back further rumors of a Christian kingdom in Africa. Henry's late brother Pedro had always maintained that this kingdom was to be found in Abyssinia, where there were known to be Christians.

MISSION TO ABYSSINIA
In May 1487 John sent out Pêro da Covilhão and Afonso de Paiva on a mission to the East. The two men traveled to Cairo and on to the Red Sea. Da Covilhão then set sail to India on an Arab ship, while Afonso headed for Abyssinia. Da

G. Dagli Orti

11

HENRY THE NAVIGATOR

The mastermind behind the first Portuguese exploits in Africa was Prince Henry of Portugal, called "the Navigator." Born in 1394, he was the third surviving son of King John I of Portugal and Philippa of Lancaster, daughter of the English John of Gaunt.

Henry was a deeply religious man. He never married, instead devoting his life to discovery. His ambition was to find the Christian kingdom of the mythical ruler Prester John, thought to be somewhere in Africa. In the small Atlantic port of Sagres he created a school of navigation, to which he invited sailors, shipbuilders, mapmakers, and merchants. Henry's sailors explored the African coast as far as the Gulf of Guinea, and he died in 1460 confident that the way to India was now open.

Dave G. Houser/Corbis

Hulton Getty

Above: Henry the Navigator, whose 15th-century envoys helped to strengthen Portuguese trading powers in West Africa.

Covilhão's voyage took him to Calicut and Goa on the Indian coast, back via Hormuz on the Persian Gulf, and along the east coast of Africa into Mozambique.

Back in Cairo, Da Covilhão found that Afonso had died. He sent his own and Afonso's reports back to Lisbon and promptly set out for Arabia, where he may have visited Mecca before sailing to Abyssinia. There he was well received by

Emperor Eksender but was forbidden to leave. Da Covilhão decided to make the best of a bad job. He settled down, married an Abyssinian wife, and spent the rest of his life at the Abyssinian court as an adviser to the emperor.

Even as Da Covilhão and Afonso were heading east, a great expedition was being prepared to head south. Its leader was Bartholomew Diaz, and in May 1488

it rounded the Cape of Good Hope, the southern tip of Africa. Meanwhile, two years previously King John had considered, and had rejected, a proposal by an Italian living in Portugal to sail west across the Atlantic. The Italian's name was Christopher Columbus. John's strategy was clearly laid out: the Portuguese would be the first to reach the Indies, and they would get there via Africa.

Above: The mighty Congo (Zaïre) River, which Diogo Cão discovered in 1482. He also explored along the river for about 100 miles (160 km).

THE MYSTERIOUS EAST

The region stretching from the eastern Mediterranean to the borders of Pakistan and India is usually referred to today as the Middle East. It is an area of deserts and arid plateaus, but parts of it are fertile, watered in the spring by the rivers carrying meltwater down from snowy peaks. The vast majority of the region's inhabitants are Muslims.

THE OTTOMAN EMPIRE

Between the 15th and early 20th centuries most of the region formed part of the Ottoman (Turkish) empire. To the east Persia (Iran) was slowly recovering from invasion by marauding nomads from the north.

The Turks captured Constantinople in 1453, and Christian Europe gradually gave up its attempts to recapture

Below: The Citadel at Aleppo. Anthony and Robert Sherley arrived at this ancient Syrian trading town in 1599 before setting out to visit the shah of Persia. Like later

explorers they traveled on camels, for the most part following established caravan routes. At night they would have to camp out in the desert beneath the stars.

Christine Osborne/Corbis

Jerusalem from the Muslims. Meanwhile the opening of the sea route to India and beyond meant that the silk and spice routes across Asia were no longer so important to traders.

However, the area to the east of the Mediterranean continued to be of interest to the Europeans. Deepening historical knowledge only increased their desire to investigate the region for themselves. For this mysterious and mystical region not only contained the holy places of the great Christian, Jewish, and Muslim religions, it was also known to be the seat of civilizations far more ancient than those of Europe itself.

THE SHERLEY BROTHERS

Before 1800 European venturers to the Middle East were few. In 1598 an English adventurer, Anthony Sherley, persuaded the Earl of Essex to send him to the court of Shah Abbas the Great of Persia. Together with his younger brother Robert, Anthony Sherley crossed the Mediterranean and arrived in the Syrian town of Aleppo in 1599.

The Middle East contained the holy places of Judaism, Christianity, and Islam.

The brothers then trekked east to the Euphrates River and followed it to the ancient city of Babylon, before proceeding to the holy city of Qum and to Isfahan. The shah welcomed the visitors and enlisted the help of Robert, who was an artilleryman, to reorganize his army.

Anthony was less fortunate. During his absence from England his patron Essex had been disgraced, and Queen Elizabeth banished Anthony Sherley from England for life. He made his way north from Persia to Moscow and spent his remaining years wandering unhappi-

MECCA—THE HOLY CITY

Mecca lies 40 miles (65 km) inland from the Red Sea port of Jedda. Since the time of the Prophet Muhammad (the founder of Islam during the seventh century) every devout Muslim has been expected to visit Mecca at least once in their lifetime.

In the heart of the holy city lies the Great Mosque. The mosque contains a dwelling that, according to the writings of Islam, was built by God before He created mankind and was later rebuilt by Abraham. The nearby village of Mina is the site where, it is said, God commanded Abraham to sacrifice his son Isaac (then forbade the slaughter at the last moment).

The holy city is banned to non-Muslims, and even today the route from Jedda to Mecca is guarded by checkpoints to prevent them entering the city. The nearby holy city of Medina is similarly closed to infidels (the faithless). Since the Middle Ages, however, inquisitive travelers from Christian countries in Europe and elsewhere have tried to penetrate the sacrosanct Islamic sites. Those few who succeeded generally cheated their way in, using heavy disguise and an assumed name.

ly around Europe. He did, however, leave behind a lengthy description of his travels in Persia to inspire future travelers.

The greatest barrier to Western exploration in the Middle East was the Ottoman government, which was unwilling to grant travel permits or to protect travelers. Mecca and the other Islamic holy cities were banned to non-Muslims, and Christian visitors might be executed if discovered.

No such barriers applied to the 17th-century Turkish traveler Celebi Eviliya. A relative of Grand Vizier Melek Ahmed Pasha, he enjoyed the favor of Sultan Murad IV and devoted the whole of his adult life to visiting the four corners of the Ottoman empire. Wherever he went, Eviliya produced copious reports for the benefit of the sultan. When published many years later, these reports filled 10 printed volumes.

The first Western scientific expedition to the area was sponsored by the king of Denmark. Six men set out from Egypt in 1761, but only one of them, the German Carsten Niebuhr, survived the journey. The expedition went east to Persia and then south through Arabia to Yemen. It kept close to the existing trade routes, and its importance lay in the high quality of the observations made by Niebuhr and his companions, which were published by Niebuhr on his return to Europe in 1767.

THE ROMANTIC AGE

The late 18th century heralded the so-called "romantic age" of Middle Eastern exploration. In Europe there was a growing interest among writers in the exotic mysticism of the region, and their idealized visions of the East fired the imagination of their readers. Travel became easier, and wealthy people sought to es-

Below: Colossal sandstone statues of Ramses II, who ruled Egypt in the 13th century B.C., guard the entrance to his tomb at Abu Simbel. Johann Burckhardt, returning from a trip down the Nile in 1813, discovered this ancient site.

Roger Wood/© Corbis

cape their ordered life within Western society—if only briefly—for the untamed wilderness offered in Arabia.

The first romantic explorer was the Swiss Johann Burckhardt, who went to London in 1806 to learn medicine. Fired with enthusiasm for travel in strange lands, he persuaded the recently founded London African Association to let him lead an expedition to Africa, but his attention was diverted to the Middle East.

Burckhardt left Malta in 1809 in the disguise of an Arab. He sailed to Aleppo and stayed in Damascus to learn Arabic. Newly disguised as a Turk, he then visited the cities of Palmyra and Baalbek. In 1812 he explored the valley of the Orontes River. Heading south in search of the biblical tomb of Aaron, he stumbled on the ruins of ancient Petra before heading for Cairo with precious notebooks and sketches concealed on his person.

In search of Aaron's tomb, Burckhardt stumbled on the ruins of ancient Petra.

From Cairo Burckhardt set out to fulfill his obligations to the London sponsors. He ascended the Nile valley to Abu Simbel and into Nubia, and turned east across Ethiopia to the Red Sea.

Mary Evans Picture Library

VISITING THE HOLY PLACES
There Burckhardt began the most dramatic part of his journey. Landing at Jedda in summer 1814, he won the confidence of the local governor and was allowed into the holy places of Mecca, Mount Arafat, and Medina. Stricken with fever in Medina, he struggled back to Cairo a year later. Weakened by illness, he spent his last years writing up very informative and accurate reports on the cities he had visited. He died in Cairo in 1817, honored with a Muslim tomb.

Above: The Swiss explorer Johann Burckhardt. A master of disguise, Burckhardt set the pattern for Europeans who were hoping to visit the holy sites of the Middle East.

Burckhardt was the prototype for many later explorers in the Middle East. Determined to learn about the history of the region and its inhabitants, he also undertook intelligence work on behalf of the British government.

BRITISH EXPEDITIONS
Burckhardt's immediate successors in the Middle East were military men. In 1819 Captain George Sadlier was sent on a diplomatic mission from India to make contact with the Egyptian Crown Prince

Below: A map showing the holy cities of Islam and ancient sites visited by European explorers. To such seasoned travelers as Richard Burton, getting into Mecca was all part of the fun of exploration.

Ibrahim Ali, then in Arabia. Ali proved elusive, however, for at every destination Sadlier found that that the prince had moved on a couple of days earlier. The exasperated captain ended up crossing the whole of Arabia from east to west—possibly becoming the first European ever to have done so.

In the 1830s James Wellstead of the British navy was commissioned to carry out surveys around the Arabian coast. In

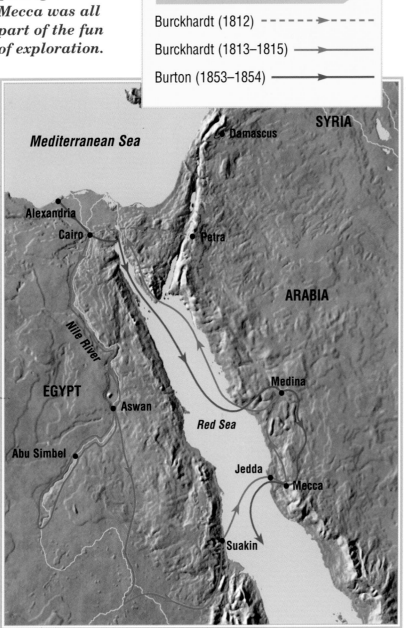

EGYPT AND ARABIA

Burckhardt (1812) ------→
Burckhardt (1813–1815) ——→
Burton (1853–1854) ——→

Mediterranean Sea

SYRIA

Damascus

Alexandria

Cairo

Petra

ARABIA

Nile River

EGYPT

Aswan

Medina

Red Sea

Abu Simbel

Jedda

Mecca

Suakin

Hulton Getty

Above: William Palgrave, who was probably the first European to cross Arabia from west to east.

the course of these he made many historical and geographical discoveries and was rewarded with a fellowship of the Royal Society in London.

SIR RICHARD BURTON

Another romantic traveler was the Englishman Sir Richard Burton, who succeeded in getting into the holy city of Mecca. He traveled from Alexandria to Medina and Mecca in 1853–1854 and managed to enter the holy cities disguised as a Muslim.

Burton later entered the British diplomatic service and in 1869 was made British consul in Damascus. He traveled widely in the East, and wrote more than 30 travel books. He also translated *The Arabian Nights*, a set of Oriental tales.

Like Burton, William Palgrave had an interest in Arab culture. After a spell in India first as a soldier and then as a

Catholic missionary, Palgrave went to Syria in 1853, where he became friends with a Maronite (Christian) community.

In 1862–1863 Palgrave crossed Arabia on a winding route that took him from Petra to the Persian Gulf. Palgrave was disguised as a Christian Arab doctor but was secretly spying for the French em-peror Napoleon III. He then returned to the British service and was involved in an abortive trip to Africa in 1865.

DOUGHTY IN DISGUISE

Charles Doughty studied geology at Cambridge University in England. In 1870 he traveled Europe before landing

Below: The Sinai Desert, which Charles Doughty visited in 1875 before traveling with the Bedouin nomads.

Steve Kaufman/Corbis

Above: The eccentric English couple Wilfrid and Anne Blunt pose in local dress with one of their beloved horses.

Mary Evans Picture Library

Abandoning disguise, Doughty lived among the Bedouin nomads for over a year. During his wanderings he explored the watercourses of the Wadi Hamd and Wadi er-Rumma. Returning to England in 1878, he wrote *Travels in Arabia Deserta*, one of the most famous books ever written about that part of the world.

Doughty was followed by another literary man, Wilfrid Blunt. Blunt shared Doughty's enthusiasm for the Arabs and in particular for the Bedouin. He and his wife Anne were passionate about horses, and in 1878–1879 they traveled widely in the northern desert of present-day Iraq, looking for thoroughbreds. A campaigner for the Arab cause, Blunt denounced Turkish rule over the area and British policy in both the Middle East and Africa.

Blunt's pro-Arab sympathies were shared by Thomas Lawrence, who went out to the Middle East in 1910 as an

at Acre in Palestine in 1875. He traveled through the Holy Land, Syria, and the Sinai Desert, disguised as a "Syrian of the middle sort of fortune." Banned from Mecca by the Turks, Doughty nevertheless joined a pilgrim caravan headed for the Islamic sites. Leaving the caravan, he then entered the desert on his own.

PETRA—CITY IN STONE

Described by the poet James Elroy Flecker as "that rose-red city, half as old as time," Petra has traces of habitation dating back to the Stone Age. It lies in a deep valley at the junction of two trade routes in what is now Jordan. Its spectacular tombs and temples are carved out of solid rock in the cliff face.

In the fourth century B.C. Petra became the capital of an Arabian people called the Nabateans. Fiercely independent, for many centuries the Nabateans resisted Greek and Roman conquest, finally yielding to the Roman emperor Trajan in A.D. 106. Petra then went into decline and was forgotten until its ruins were discovered and identified by Johann Burckhardt in 1812.

Right: Royal tombs at Petra in Jordan. Johann Burckhardt discovered the ancient city while traveling from Syria to Cairo.

Mary Evans Picture Library

David Joyner/Popperfoto

Above: Gertrude Bell, the English traveler and politician, picnicking with King Faisal of Iraq in 1922.

archeologist. When the First World War broke out in 1914, Lawrence joined the British Army. He used his knowledge of the area and its people to stir up an Arab revolt against the Turks. The revolt succeeded, but Jordan and Iraq then came under British control. "Lawrence of Arabia," as he was known, felt that he had been manipulated and left the army.

AN ENGLISHWOMAN IN THE DESERT

Another explorer caught up in politics was Gertrude Bell. The daughter of an English industrialist, she went to Persia in 1892 and learned Farsi (the modern Persian language). In 1899 she went to Damascus to learn Arabic and decided to become an explorer. Traveling alone in the desert was dangerous for women, and it was some years before she plucked up the courage to leave the beaten track.

In 1910–1911 Bell trekked across the Syrian desert to Iraq and two years later journeyed to Ha´il in the Arabian desert. Returning to Damascus, she volunteered for war work assisting the Arabs. Bell stayed on after the war and became a leading figure in local politics, known among her jealous colleagues as "the uncrowned queen of Iraq."

A CONVERT TO ISLAM

One admirer of Bell was Harry Philby, father of the British double-agent Kim Philby. Harry first went to Arabia in the 1910s and converted to Islam. He probably covered more ground in eastern and southern Arabia than any other explorer.

In 1917 Philby crossed from Bahrain on the Persian Gulf via Riyadh to Jedda on the Red Sea. The following year he

THE EMPTY QUARTER

Inland from the south coast of Arabia lie two contrasting areas. On the western side, in Yemen, is the fertile Wadi Hadramawt. It was first explored by the German archeologist Leo Hirsch in the 1890s and is almost the only part of Arabia with enough rain to support a permanent river.

To the northeast of the wadi is the desolate and rainless Rub `al Khali, or Empty Quarter. It is the largest continuous sand desert in the world, 250,000 square miles (647,500 square km) in extent and virtually uninhabited.

The Empty Quarter remained unexplored until Bertram Thomas crossed it in 1930–1931. He was followed in 1932 by the veteran Harry Philby and in the 1940s by Wilfrid Thesiger. But it remains as empty and mysterious as ever.

Below: Windswept dunes of the Ramlat Desert in Saudi Arabia, at the southwestern corner of the immense Empty Quarter.

Arthur Thevenart/Corbis

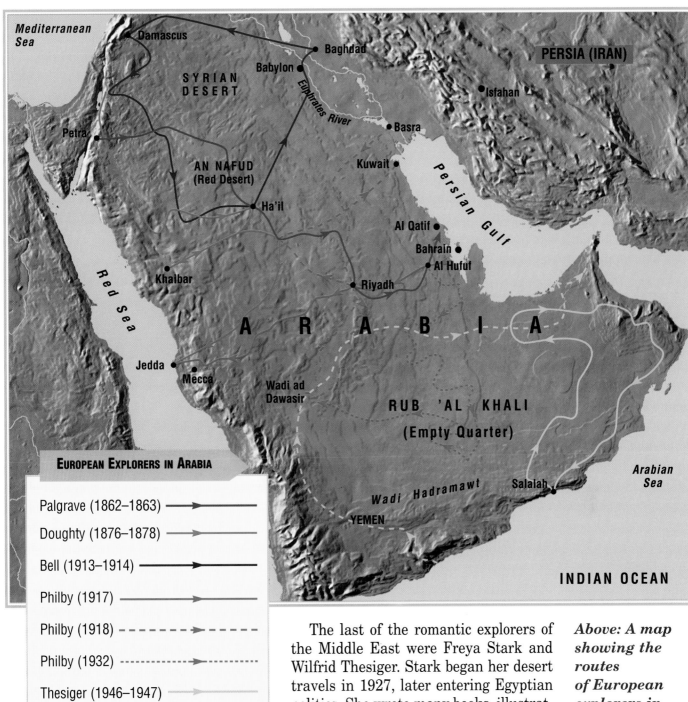

EUROPEAN EXPLORERS IN ARABIA

Palgrave (1862–1863) ⟶

Doughty (1876–1878) ⟶

Bell (1913–1914) ⟶

Philby (1917) ⟶

Philby (1918) ‐ ‐ ‐ ➔

Philby (1932) ·············➔

Thesiger (1946–1947) ⟶

Thesiger (1947–1948) ‐ ‐ ‐ ⟶

The last of the romantic explorers of the Middle East were Freya Stark and Wilfrid Thesiger. Stark began her desert travels in 1927, later entering Egyptian politics. She wrote many books, illustrated with her own photographs, about the culture and landscape of the region. For his part Thesiger was drawn to the wilderness. In the 1940s he twice crossed the Empty Quarter in search of a world unspoiled by civilization.

In 1938 the first petroleum deposits were discovered in the Arabian peninsula; since then exploration in the region has concentrated on the search for oil.

Above: A map showing the routes of European explorers in Arabia. The area had a powerful attraction for Europeans seeking excitement and adventure.

traveled from Basra at the head of the Gulf to Riyadh; from there he looped down to the Wadi ad Dawasir and back to Riyadh before returning to the coast near Kuwait. Then in 1932 Philby traversed a large section of the notoriously bleak Empty Quarter in the far south.

Exploring NORTH AFRICA

Inland of the African coast bordering the Mediterranean Sea, a small fertile stretch soon gives way to the wastelands of the Sahara, the world's largest desert. Only the Nile valley to the east gives easy overland access to the rest of Africa.

For a long time the only travelers across the vast desert were Arab and Berber camel trains in search of gold and slaves. In this harsh country temperatures can rise by day to 130° F (54° C) and fall again to freezing by night, and blinding sandstorms can bury people and animals within hours.

Western exploration of the Sahara began in earnest in 1788, with the foundation of the London-based African Association. The Association immediately sent out an explorer, John Ledyard, to Egypt, with a brief to cross the desert southward and westward to find the mysterious Niger River. There was a keen desire to find out whether the Niger flowed east or west, and whether it emptied into the Atlantic or into the Nile or just petered out in the desert.

Ledyard died before starting his trip, and his place was taken by Friedrich Hornemann in 1798. Hornemann headed west as far as Murzuk in the Fezzan (in southern Libya) but could get no further and turned back to Tripoli on the

The Berbers (below) and the Arabs trekked the Sahara for centuries before the arrival of Europeans.

Patrick Ward/Corbis

Nik Wheeler/Corbis

Hulton Getty

Above: Dixon Denham, who journeyed in search of the Niger River (left) during the 1820s.

Mediterranean coast. He tried again and according to some reports actually reached the Niger, but he died in the desert without being able to send back any report of his achievement. For the time being the mystery of the Niger remained unsolved.

War between Britain and France delayed further exploration in North Africa for a number of years. In 1819 two Englishmen—Joseph Ritchie, a young surgeon and poet, and a naval officer named George Lyon—set out from Tripoli into the Sahara. Hopelessly ill-equipped, they got as far as Murzuk where they fell victim to dysentery. Only Lyon survived, returning desperately ill but with a full report on the Fezzan.

SEARCHING FOR THE SOURCE

In 1821 two Scotsmen, Walter Oudney and Hugh Clapperton, set out on a better-equipped expedition in Ritchie and Lyon's footsteps. They were joined at Murzuk by an Englishman, Major Dixon Denham, and pushed on to the south across the desert, reaching the shores of

e. t. archive

Lake Chad in February 1823. There they parted. Denham explored around the lake, while Oudney and Clapperton headed west, still searching for the source of the elusive Niger.

Oudney succumbed to pneumonia in 1824, but Clapperton rejoined Denham, and the two trekked back to Tripoli, arriving back in England in 1825. The trip had been marked by difficult relations with the tribesmen they met en route and by personal tensions between the two Scotsmen and the English major.

Luckily Oudney was both a good diplomat and a good observer, and his diary, together with that of Denham, produced a detailed record of the variety of country the expedition had crossed.

Another British explorer, Major Alexander Laing, succeeded in roughly locating the source of the Niger River in 1824. The next year Laing crossed the Sahara Desert, and reached Timbuktu, the first European to do so in modern times. But on his way back he was captured and killed by Tuareg nomads.

Above: An African village under attack, sketched by Dixon Denham during his explorations around the region of Lake Chad in 1823.

In 1849 the German-born explorers Heinrich Barth and Adolf Overweg joined a British-sponsored expedition to the Sahara led by the Englishman James Richardson. In 1850 they trekked to Murzuk and then crossed the Sahara on a new route to the west of the one chosen by Oudney and his companions.

Richardson died of a fever on the southbound journey, and Barth assumed command. He and Overweg systematically explored the whole area around Lake Chad. They mapped the shifting shoreline of the lake and the rivers that flowed into it and made notes on the culture of the region's inhabitants.

A year after Richardson's death Overweg also died of disease, and Barth carried on alone. Reaching Say on the Niger, he trekked overland to Timbuktu, returning downriver by boat. Barth was then joined by yet another German, Dr. Vogel, who took over the task of exploring the area south of Lake Chad. However, Vogel was killed by natives while attempting to travel east to the Nile valley.

Barth returned to London alone nearly six years after first setting out. His exploits set new standards in exploration. His description of his travels, published in the late 1850s, covered every aspect of what he had seen, from geography and botany to history and linguistics.

THE FRENCH IN ALGERIA

Sensing that Arab power in the Mediterranean was on the wane, the French had invaded Algeria in 1830.

Below: Heinrich Barth's team encamped in the forest in 1852. Barth was an exemplary explorer who took an interest in every aspect of the regions of Africa through which he traveled.

Mary Evans Picture Library

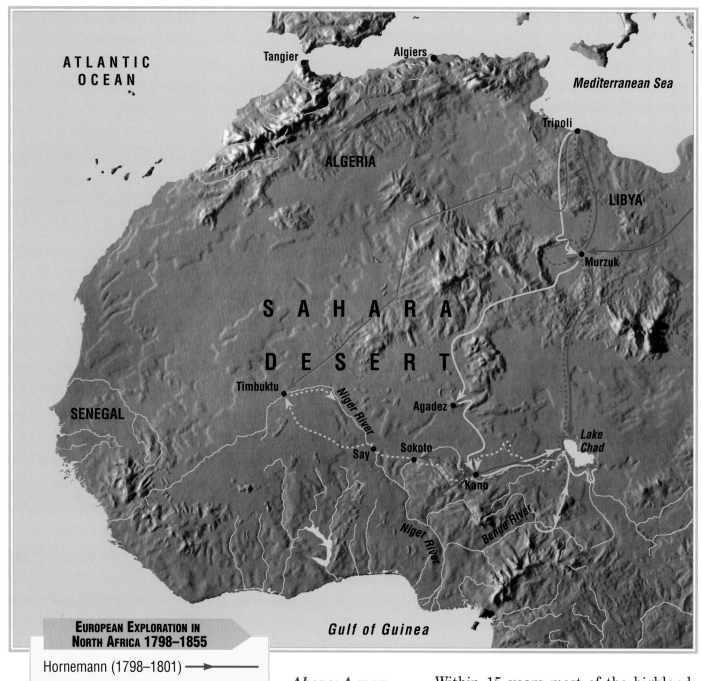

EUROPEAN EXPLORATION IN NORTH AFRICA 1798–1855

Hornemann (1798–1801) ⟶

● Death of Hornemann

Oudney, Clapperton, Denham (1821–1825) ⇢

Laing (1825–26) ⟶

Barth

(1850–1852) ⟶

(1852–1855) ⇢

Above: A map showing the European expeditions across North Africa in the late 18th and early 19th centuries.

Within 15 years most of the highlands north of the Sahara proper had been subjugated, and in 1848 the whole of Algeria was declared part of France. This was the first of many moves by the Western powers that were to change the face of African exploration, both promoting it and distorting its aims for political gain.

French explorers now began a pincer movement into the western Sahara, heading south from the Mediterranean and north from Senegal in the west.

In 1857 the French explorer Henri Duveyrier rode into the Sahara from Algiers and forged close ties with the Tuareg peoples, a nomadic people of Berber descent. On his return to France he published a dictionary of the Berber language. Duveyrier went back to Africa in 1859 and accompanied a Tuareg camel caravan into south-central Algeria. An expedition across the Sahara in 1860 took him deep into the Tuaregs' desert homeland, where he lived with the locals for over a year. He had the support of Napoleon III, who wanted to establish friendly ties with the Tuareg.

GERHARD ROHLFS
The most successful explorer in the French service at that time was actually a German, Gerhard Rohlfs. A doctor with

Below: The vast rolling sand dunes and scrub of the Algerian Sahara Desert, which Henri Duveyrier explored in the 1850s–1860s.

Dave G. Houser/Corbis

the French Foreign Legion in Algeria from 1855, he abandoned his career in 1861 to be an explorer.

Rohlfs's first travels, beginning in 1862, took him through the area south of the Atlas Mountains. A first attempt to cross the Sahara failed, but in 1865 he tried again. Reaching Lake Chad, he found his way to the Benue River. He sailed down it to where it joined the Niger and then on to the sea.

> ## Rohlfs was a doctor with the French Foreign Legion in Algeria during the 1850s.

Rohlfs returned to North Africa in 1869 and again in 1873–1874 to explore the northern and eastern fringes of the Libyan desert. In 1878 he set out across the Sahara between Lake Chad and the Nile but gave up in Kufra. Rohlfs ended his days as German consul in Zanzibar.

Although medically trained, Rohlfs was not a scientist. Oskar Lenz, however, was. His trip to Timbuktu from Morocco in 1880 covered no new ground, but he was the first person to make thorough geological observations and explain many features of the Saharan terrain.

For a long time Vogel and Rohlfs were almost the only Saharan explorers to show an interest in the desert's eastern fringe where it descends toward the Nile. In the 1860s a few explorers ventured up the Bahr el-Ghazal, a western tributary of the White Nile, and entered the area separating the Nile and Congo basins. But the connection between these areas and the eastern Sahara was only made by Gustav Nachtigal in the 1870s.

Gerhard Rohlfs (right, seated) crossed the Sahara from north to south in 1865; 30 years later Jean Marchand (below) led a west–east expedition across North Africa from the Congo River to the Nile.

Popperfoto

Mary Evans Picture Library

Nachtigal's work on the Congo watershed was completed by Wilhelm Junker in the early 1880s. Junker was the first European to prove that the Uele was in fact part of the Congo River system and not, as Nachtigal thought, linked with the Niger. With that discovery the decisive mapping of the northern half of the African continent was completed.

THE FRENCH TAKE CONTROL

French ambitions in North Africa included plans for a railroad across the Sahara to the Niger and beyond. In 1880 and 1881 Paul Flatters was sent out to survey the route. Three French explorers, including Flatters, were killed by tribesmen in the course of these attempts. Accordingly, the French despatched military escorts for their surveyors, which soon led to outright military occupation of the whole area.

The expedition that sealed French control of the entire territory from the Mediterranean to the Congo basin was

Nachtigal was a scientific explorer in the mold of Barth and Lenz. In his journeys across the Sahara, starting in 1869, he became the first European to explore the mountainous Tibesti region in northern Chad, close to the Libyan border.

Nachtigal became the first European to explore the mountains of Tibesti.

He also succeeded where Vogel and Rohlfs had failed in crossing from Chad to the Nile. While making forays to the south of Lake Chad he explored the Uele River, which had been discovered by the German botanist Georg Schweinfurth a few years earlier. Nachtigal returned to Germany in 1875 after nearly six years in the desert.

THE FRENCH FOREIGN LEGION

When France invaded Algeria in 1830, one of the first acts of the king, Louis-Philippe, was to establish a military corps on the new territory. This was the *Légion Etrangère*, or Foreign Legion.

The Algerian unit, based at Sidi bel Abbès, was staffed by French officers but drew its ranks from foreign mercenaries. However, the fighting men were promised full French citizenship after serving an enlistment of five years. Many of the legionnaires were ex-convicts for whom the Legion promised a clean slate in return for their unconditional loyalty. Despite the tough conditions, the soldiers still preferred to wear the famous *képi blanc* (white cap) of the Legion, symbol of strict discipline and professionalism, to service in a regular army. Today the Legion is open to French citizens in addition to foreign recruits. Over the years its forces have served as far afield as Spain, Italy, and Mexico.

For more than a century the Foreign Legion played a key role in protecting France's North African territories. In 1962 it moved its base to France in preparation for Algeria's independence.

LIFE ON A DESERT CARAVAN

Before the advent of the automobile the only way to cross the African and Arabian deserts was by camel caravan. Progress across the bleak wastes was painfully slow, and there were many hazards in store for travelers—Westerners in particular.

Temperatures were blisteringly hot by day, falling to freezing point by night. In a sandstorm, which could strike at any moment, the traveler simply had to lie flat and cover up until the winds died down again. The Englishman William Palgrave, visiting Arabia in 1862, likened sandstorms to "Hell, but without the eternity."

Charles Doughty, who accompanied some 6,000 pilgrims journeying to Mecca in 1876, described marches that lasted a day and a night. He returned to Damascus with the native Bedouin tribesmen, who made "horrid sounds" with their music and nursed sick pilgrims with a brew of asses' dung and milk. The Bedouin also, apparently, toyed briefly with the idea of killing Doughty. The caravan was beset at one point by bandits, who stole several camels. In the end the terrible heat and desolation, the "wilderness of burning and rusty horror of unformed matter," cost Doughty his health and almost his life.

Tuareg nomads (below) still continue the centuries-old tradition of crossing the Sahara Desert with camel trains.

led from the north by Fernand Foureau. It set out in 1900 in the wake of the transcontinental journey by Jean-Baptiste Marchand northeastward from the Congo to the Nile.

The expedition got off to a bad start, losing almost all its camels after a few days.

Foureau had already made a number of expeditions into the Algerian interior but had never gone the full distance across the Sahara. This time his instructions were to lead a massive expedition—with military support—to converge at Lake Chad, with other French expeditions coming from the Niger in the west and the Congo in the south.

The expedition got off to a bad start, losing almost all its camels within a few days. But it regrouped and carried on to its planned meeting place. Having made the rendezvous, Foureau continued down to the mouth of the Congo River. He de-

Barbara Maurer/Getty Images

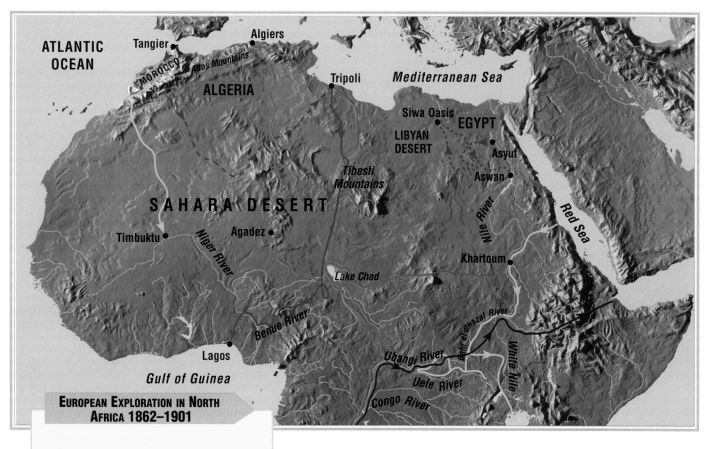

EUROPEAN EXPLORATION IN NORTH AFRICA 1862–1901

Rohlfs (1862–1864)   ‑ ‑ ‑ ‑ ‑ ►‑ ‑

Rohlfs (1865–1867)   ————►

Rohlfs (1873–1874)   ‑‑‑‑‑‑‑‑►‑‑‑

Nachtigal (1869–1874)   ————►

Junker (1879–1883)   ————►

Lenz (1880)   ————►

Marchand (1898)   ————►

Foureau (1900–1901)   ————►

lost their lives, killed by locals or struck down by disease. The communities and cultures of the African peoples came under threat from the Europeans. And the Arab and Berber peoples lost their independence at the end of the century, when exploration turned to conquest.

The exploration of North Africa cost many lives and caused political upheaval.

The north coast of Africa received a massive influx of French, and later Italian, settlers, although few Europeans settled in the desert regions. European trade with southern, western, and eastern Africa continued to be directed toward the coast. The rich culture of the interior of Africa where Arab and black African influences meet remained little known in the West for many years.

Above: European routes across North Africa in the mid- to late 19th century. This was a period when explorers and their political backers turned to the northeast, seeking to fill in the blanks on the map between the Congo and Nile rivers.

voted much time to geographical and biological observations. The standard set by Foureau was to be followed by many later explorers in the French service.

COUNTING THE COST
The exploration of North Africa during the 18th and 19th centuries was not achieved without cost. Many explorers

Pioneers in South Africa

The sparsely populated southern tip of Africa, with its pleasant climate and fertile plains, began to be settled by Europeans in the 17th century. Soon after the Dutch began to challenge the Portuguese in trade with the East Indies, the Dutch East India Company was es-tablished. In 1652 it set up a staging post at Cape Town, and this soon developed into a small but prosperous colony. In the 18th century European botanists visited the area, eager to compare its flora with that of the Mediterranean. They brought new plants back to Europe to supply the growing craze for botanical gardens.

The early Dutch settlers did not venture far from the coast. In 1736, however, an expedition inland made contact with the Bantu, a Central African people who were gradually expanding southward, displacing the native Eushmen and Hottentots. A fight broke out, and the

Below: The rugged cliffs known as "The Twelve Apostles" are a distinctive feature of the landscape around Cape Town—where Dutch traders established a thriving colony in the 1650s.

Patrick Ward/Corbis

Dutch were repulsed. A few years later in 1752 August Beutler led a pioneering party eastward along the south coast, returning by an inland route and bringing back precious geographical information.

By 1800 travelers had ventured as far north as the Orange River and the edge of the Kalahari Desert. During the war against Napoleon the British occupied the Cape, which was granted to them by treaty in 1815. English and Scottish missionaries flooded in to join groups such as the Moravian Brethren. A second wave of naturalists came too, of whom the most important was William Burchell.

Mary Evans Picture Library

Above: The British traveler and missionary John Campbell, who explored the Kalahari Desert and several rivers, including the Orange, Vaal, and Limpopo between 1812 and 1821.

Burchell's travels in the South African interior in 1811–1812 yielded a portfolio of several beautifully executed drawings of the landscape and its plants, animals, and peoples. But it was a missionary, the Rev. John Campbell, who ventured farthest inland. In 1813 he plotted the course of the west-flowing Orange River; returning in 1819, he reached the source of the east-flowing Limpopo River.

THE GREAT TREK

Conflicts soon arose between the Dutch settlers and the British newcomers, particularly the missionaries. The Dutch held that slavery was justified by the

Shaen Adey; ABPL/Corbis

Popperfoto

Bible; the British denied this. When the British moved to abolish slavery in the province, the Dutch farmers (the Boers) decided to leave. Preparations began in 1833, and by 1836 hundred of settlers were on the march; the Great Trek of the Boers had begun.

On foot and in lumbering ox-carts, men, women, and children trekked through the barren mountains, sleeping under the open skies. Once in the interior they divided: some headed northeast into Natal, while others took a more northerly route across the Vaal River into what became known as Transvaal.

Immediately the Boers met strong opposition from the Zulu and Matabele tribes. After fierce fighting the Matabele king Mzilikazi was driven north across the Limpopo River in 1837.

The following year in Natal the Zulu king Dingaan prepared a trap for the Boers, enticing their leader Piet Retief to

Left: Natal in southern Africa. These rolling hills became home for many of the Boers who resented British domination in the Cape. Between 1833 and 1850 the Boers headed out on the Great Trek (below)—an epic exodus by ox train into the Orange Free State, Natal, and the Transvaal.

his camp and murdering him. Under a new leader, Andries Pretorius, the Dutch then drew the Zulus into their own trap. Lashing their wagons together to form a stockade, they took up elephant guns and lay in wait for the Zulu warriors.

A terrible slaughter ensued. The Zulus did not have firearms, or even bows and arrows. They had to advance on foot, with only their shields to protect them. They were mowed down under a hail of Boer bullets. After the massacre the Boers settled down to farm their land, which was officially granted to them by treaty 15 years later.

ROBERT MOFFAT

Relations between the British and the Matabele were more peaceable. Credit for that is due to the Scottish missionary Robert Moffat, who was sent out to South

Africa by the London Missionary Society in 1817. Moffat first journeyed north from Cape Town through desert country inhabited by small numbers of Bushmen.

Deciding that missionary work would be more fruitful elsewhere, in 1821 Moffat and his wife set up a base at Kuruman, near Matabele country. Moffat established friendly relations with King Mzilikazi, who granted protection to the British missionaries at work in the lands over which he had influence.

Profiting from this security, Moffat himself traveled widely in the area north of the Vaal River throughout the 1820s and made an extensive survey of the Orange River system to supplement the work already done by John Campbell.

DAVID LIVINGSTONE

In 1841 Moffat was joined at Kuruman by another Scotsman, David Livingstone. The son of a poor family, Livingstone had gone to work in the cotton mills at the age of 10 but had nevertheless managed to qualify as a doctor. He came out to Africa full of zeal to spread the word of God and to fight the evils of slavery.

But Livingstone was not satisfied with routine missionary activity. He did not want to stay at Kuruman, instructing converts in their new religion. He set up a new mission station at Mabotse and married Moffat's daughter Mary in 1844. His new ambition was to be an explorer.

In 1849 Livingstone persuaded two wealthy big-game hunters to fund and accompany him on an expedition across the eastern side of the Kalahari as far as Lake Ngami. The explorers and their native guides trekked by wagon across the desert for two months. Assailed by thirst and stung by venomous scorpions, they reached the lake in August.

In 1850 Livingstone began a second trip, hoping to meet the chief of the Makalolo at the Chobe River where it joins the Zambezi. His first attempt was

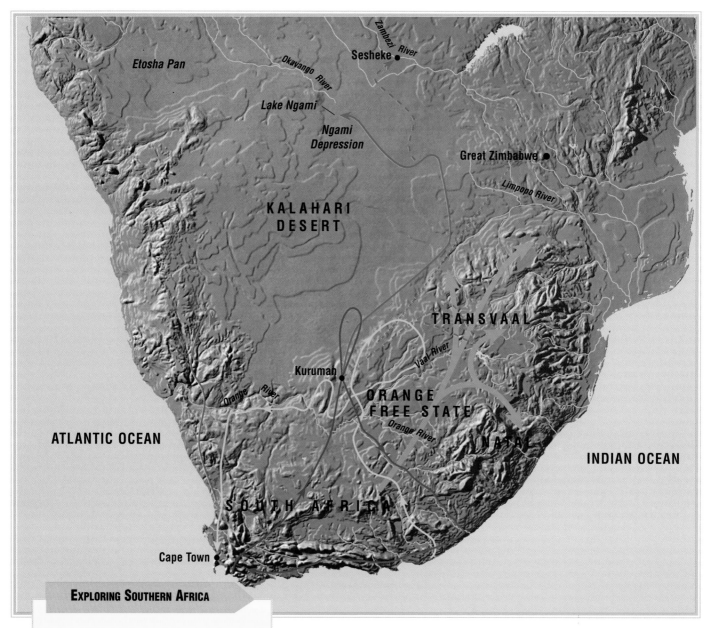

Map labels:
- Etosha Pan
- Zambezi River
- Okavango River
- Sesheke
- Lake Ngami
- Ngami Depression
- Great Zimbabwe
- Limpopo River
- KALAHARI DESERT
- TRANSVAAL
- Vaal River
- Kuruman
- ORANGE FREE STATE
- Orange River
- Orange River
- NATAL
- ATLANTIC OCEAN
- INDIAN OCEAN
- SOUTH AFRICA
- Cape Town

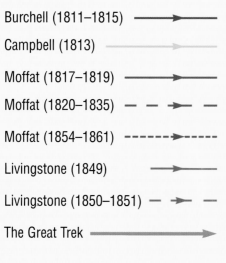

EXPLORING SOUTHERN AFRICA

Burchell (1811–1815)	⟶
Campbell (1813)	⟶
Moffat (1817–1819)	⟶
Moffat (1820–1835)	– – ⟶ –
Moffat (1854–1861)	----⟶----
Livingstone (1849)	⟶
Livingstone (1850–1851)	– ⟶ –
The Great Trek	⟶

Above: Inroads into southern Africa in the 19th century. Missionaries made the first expeditions, and some of them became eager explorers.

not successful, but he tried again in 1851, taking his wife and children with him. They met the chief and reached the mighty Zambezi River near Sesheke.

Livingstone's sights were now firmly set on Central Africa, and his exploits in the years that followed were to take him deep into the heart of the continent.

Back in Kuruman, Moffat continued to run his mission. He spent his evenings laboriously translating the Bible into the Sechuana language. However, he longed to meet Mzilikazi again and in spite of his advancing years made two journeys

MARY LIVINGSTONE

Mary Livingstone (right) was the eldest child of the Rev. Robert Moffat and his wife (also named Mary). She was born in 1821 at an isolated mission station in South Africa, where her parents, both Methodist missionaries from Manchester in England, had moved the previous year.

In 1844 the young Mary Moffat married David Livingstone. Six years later she and her three children joined him on a trek across the desert, braving crocodiles, scorpions, and tsetse flies. On their return Mary gave birth to a child, who died in infancy. The following year they set out again, and this time a child was born on the journey. Mary took the children to Cape Town and then to England.

In 1858 Mary agreed to come back to Africa with David and join him on part of one his trips in the Great Lakes region. On April 11, 1862, she boarded the boat to take her upstream. Within a few days she was struck down by fever, and on the 27th she died.

Mary Livingstone was a courageous traveler with a pioneering spirit and became one of the first white women to penetrate south-central Africa.

Mary Evans Picture Library

into the region beyond the Limpopo where Mzilikazi and the Matebele had settled after being driven north by the Boers. On his trip in 1854 Moffat gave the king a package of papers to hand over to Livingstone, who was exploring in the Zambezi valley a couple of hundred miles away to the north. The Matabele passed the package to the Makalolo, and it reached Livingstone the following year.

Meanwhile, in 1850 Francis Galton, an amateur scientist, had landed in the southwest. He and his assistant Charles Andersson planned to head east across the Kalahari to Lake Ngami. Blocked by tribes, they turned north into the Etosha Pan in Ovamboland before being forced back. Galton returned to England in 1852, but Andersson stayed on. In 1853–1854 he battled through to Lake Ngami; three years later he reached the Okavango River near the Angolan border.

COLONIAL AFRICA

By 1860 the map of southern Africa was acquiring a new shape. Geographers knew the main features of the landscape, and the European nations were marking out zones of influence in the region. The British had control of Cape Province and Natal. Boer settlers of Dutch origins held the Transvaal and the Orange Free State

Below: David Livingstone reaches Lake Ngami during his expedition of 1849.

Mary Evans Picture Library

saw. A granite wall 800 feet (240 m) long and 30 feet (9 m) high surrounded large huts, compounds, and a mysterious conical tower. Objects found inside included fragments of Chinese porcelain.

Great Zimbabwe was clear proof that African civilization was not all primitive but had reached a high material and cultural level. This came as a jolt to Europeans. A British colonial official, Richard Hall, invented a theory to prove that Zimbabwe had been built not by Africans but by invaders from elsewhere.

SCIENTISTS, HUNTERS, AND TRADERS
As white men continued the settlement of southern Africa, they made inroads into even the most remote areas. Many

Above: African villagers performing a welcome ceremony for David Livingstone in 1860.

in the interior. German missionaries and scientists were active in present-day Namibia, where they set up a colony.

Farther north the Portuguese had bases in Angola on the west coast and Mozambique on the east. For a while the Portuguese entertained notions of making a link across the continent.

In 1802 an expedition under Pedro Baptista had set out from Angola to make its way east. The expedition certainly got as far as the Zambezi and may have reached Mozambique. If so, it would have been the first European crossing of the continent. But there was no followup. Angola and Mozambique remained separated, and it was the British, rather than the Portuguese, who were to spearhead exploration into the heart of Africa.

THE LOST CITY OF ZIMBABWE
During this northward push European explorers first came on the ruined city of Great Zimbabwe, north of the Limpopo. At first they could not believe what they

explorers, particularly the Germans and the Czech Dr. Holub, were scientists, interested both in the land and its wildlife and also in its people. By the 1900s a new type of scientist had made an appearance: the professional anthropologist. The traditions of native African peoples began at last to be understood, even as they were vanishing forever in the wake of colonization.

Alongside those who came to study Africa's wonders came the hunters. Unlike the missionaries, who mostly came from poor backgrounds, big-game hunters tended to be wealthy men. They shot at animals for sport rather than for trade and could afford to mount lavish expeditions in search of their quarry.

e. t. archive

Above: African women making pottery in the early 1800s. Scenes such as these reinforced the opinion of British colonials that Africans had a uniformly primitive culture. But the discovery of the ancient citadel at Great Zimbabwe (left), with its evidence of a cultural heritage dating back 1,000 years, forced Europeans to think again.

It was two such big-game hunters, Mungo Murray and William Oswell, who financed David Livingstone's first expedition to Lake Ngami.

After them came other hunters such as Frederick Selous, who made repeated trips in search of big game in the country between Lake Ngami and the Zambezi River in the 1870s and 1880s, reaching as far as the Mozambique coast at Beira. In 1890 Selous turned colonist and led a group of pioneers to seize Matabeleland for the British.

Gold was found north of the Limpopo in 1860, bringing prospectors into the area.

A lot of interest in exploration, however, was connected with trade—ivory, for example, from elephant tusks. Gold in small quantities was discovered north of the Limpopo River in 1860, followed by much larger deposits in the Transvaal to the south, bringing prospectors into the area. South Africa is now one of the world's largest producers of gold.

THE ROMANCE
OF THE
NILE

The Nile is the world's longest river. From the source of the White Nile in the Great Lakes region of Africa to where it reaches the Mediterranean Sea at Alexandria, the Nile flows over 4,100 miles (6,500 km), making it 200 miles (320 km) longer than either the Amazon

Farrell Grehan/Corbis

or the Mississippi–Missouri. In ancient times there were many legends about its source, and in the Middle Ages Arab travelers ventured a long way up its course into the Sudan. To find the source of the Nile became one of the great obsessions of European explorers.

Hulton Getty

Above: In 1770 James Bruce toasted King George III of England at what he thought to be the source of the Nile. He had in fact only traced the Blue Nile, the easterly of the Nile's two main branches. Bruce was publicly ridiculed on his return to Britain.

Left: The Nile in Egypt. To discover the source of this mighty river became the obsession of many European explorers in Africa.

Between the Red Sea and the Nile valley lies the mainly Christian country of Ethiopia, which had been visited by the Portuguese Afonso de Paiva and Pedro da Covilhão in the 1480s. Following in their footsteps, Jesuit missionaries entered the area from 1550 onward.

In 1589 a Portuguese Jesuit in India, Pedro Paez, embarked for Africa to join in the work of assisting the Christians in Ethiopia. On his way he was captured and enslaved by Arab pirates, and it was not until 1603 that he finally reached his destination. In the course of his travels in Ethiopia in 1613 he found the source of a river that flowed through the Ethiopian mountains toward Khartoum.

Paez's discovery was confirmed 10 years later by another Portuguese Jesuit, Jerónimo Lobo. After many adventures Lobo returned to Portugal in 1636 and wrote a dramatic account of his travels, which was soon translated into English, Italian, and French.

JAMES BRUCE

In 1768 James Bruce, an explorer who claimed descent from the Scottish hero Robert Bruce, set out from Cairo to explore Ethiopia. He found the great Tisisat Falls and a source for the river

Kennan Ward Photography/Corbis

Portuguese side and treated Bruce as a fraud. In truth he had not, as he had claimed, found the source of the Nile. His discovery was merely the Blue Nile, a tributary of the Nile. And Bruce had been no nearer to the true source of that river than the two Jesuits a century earlier. Nevertheless, his lengthy account of his travels, with illustrations by his Italian colleague Luigi Balugani, was a mine of valuable information about the area.

After the brief controversy aroused by Bruce, interest in the Nile faded for a while. When it revived, the approach taken was from a very different direction.

REBMANN AND KRAPF

In the 1840s the Church Missionary Society set up an outpost on the East African coast near Zanzibar. Arab traders were active in the area, and from them the missionaries heard that great lakes or inland seas existed in the interior. With the aid of a Swahili guide the German missionaries Johann Krapf and Johann Rebmann made a series of journeys in search of these lakes.

In 1848 Rebmann became the first white man to glimpse the snows of Mount Kilimanjaro. The two missionaries then joined up to explore further, and in 1849 Krapf became the first European to sight Mount Kenya. The reports they sent back to London's Royal Geographical Society (R.G.S.) describing the snow-capped peaks caused great astonishment, stimulating interest in the region and paving the way for further exploration.

BURTON TAKES UP THE CHALLENGE

In 1853 the English adventurer Richard Burton, fresh from his visit to the Islamic holy city of Mecca in Arabia, met Krapf in Cairo and was inspired by the missionary's report.

Richard Burton proposed to the R.G.S. a more thorough exploration beginning on the east coast. The R.G.S. realized

higher up. Seeing some high mountains nearby, he decided they must be the Mountains of the Moon believed by the ancient geographer Ptolemy to lie at the source of the Nile.

On his return to London in 1774 Bruce found himself at the center of a storm. In his account of his travels he had poured scorn on the exploits of the Portuguese who had been there before him. To his horror, many people in England took the

In 1848 the German Johann Rebmann became the first European to see Kilimanjaro (above), an extinct volcano in Tanzania and Africa's highest peak.

that Burton's plan had strategic importance. They consulted the government, which agreed to lend support. The R.G.S. told Burton to search for a vast lake reported to be somewhere in East Africa. Then "you are to proceed northward toward the range of mountains marked on our maps as containing the probable source of the Nile, which it will be your next great object to discover."

The differences between Burton and Speke were later to erupt into hatred.

Between his meeting with Krapf and putting forward his plan to the R.G.S., Burton made a side trip to Somaliland. He took as his lieutenants three young officers from the Indian Army. The party was ambushed by Somalis. One of the young officers was killed, and Burton and another officer, John Speke, barely escaped with their lives.

AN ILL-FATED PARTNERSHIP
After this baptism of fire Burton decided to take Speke with him on the journey to the Nile. Before very long the two men found that they had little in common. Burton was an intellectual, fascinated by exotic cultures; Speke liked shooting game. The differences between them were later to erupt into outright hatred.

Burton and Speke arrived in East Africa early in 1857. Despite contrary advice from Rebmann, Burton chose to follow the Arab caravan route inland from the coast to the trading center at Tabora. Burton knew and loved the Arabs. He also knew that other explorers had come to grief by provoking their hostility, and he was determined not to follow suit.

With the Africans, however, Burton was less successful. He and Speke took on 100 African porters; they set out from

Below: John Hanning Speke, British soldier and hunter. Richard Burton chose Speke to accompany him on his 1857 expedition to find the source of the Nile, but the two men were widely different in character and soon fell out.

Bagamoyo on the coast in June and took over four months to reach Tabora, which was 500 miles (800 km) inland. Many porters deserted, and at Tabora the rest refused to go on. Burton and Speke were both suffering from malaria.

With help from the Arabs in Tabora and from his caravan leader Sidi Bombay, Burton reorganized his caravan and carried on. On February 13, 1858, he found himself overlooking the pale blue waters of Lake Tanganyika. Could these be the headwaters of the Nile?

Burton and Speke began to explore the northern end of the lake by canoe. The boatmen refused to go to the end, and Burton was too ill to carry on without them. The two explorers returned to

Hulton Getty

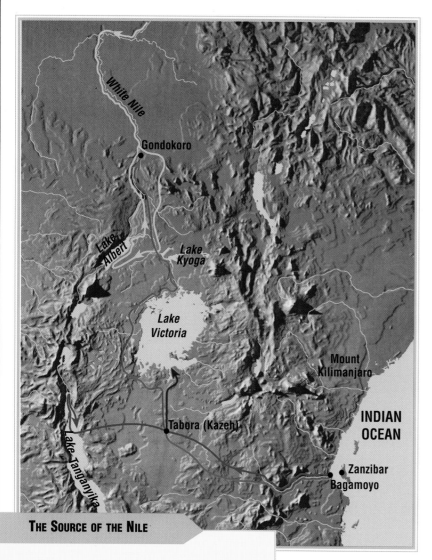

An argument flared up between the two explorers. Burton thought that the Nile began at Lake Tanganyika. Speke thought that its source lay in Lake Victoria and that the water from Lake Tanganyika drained out on the southern side and not to the north. The two headed back to the coast, quarreling bitterly.

They reached Zanzibar on the east coast early in 1859. Burton was too sick to travel any further, so Speke returned to England without him. Burton followed two weeks later, to discover that Speke had already presented his own version of events to the Royal Geographical Society. The next expedition, the R.G.S. decided, should be led by Speke, and Burton would have no part in it.

Burton returned to find that Speke had already told his account of the journey.

Burton had every reason to feel aggrieved. By addressing the R.G.S. on his own Speke had broken an agreement that the two men would present their results together. Morally, therefore, Speke was in the wrong—but geographically he was correct.

As Speke suspected, the Nile flows out of Lake Victoria to the north, and its headwaters are the small rivers that feed into the lake. Lake Tanganyika, on the other hand, drains southward—as the two men would have discovered had they reached the head of the lake where the Rusizi River flows into it. Speke's new expedition set out to turn his beliefs about Lake Victoria into a certainty.

SPEKE AND GRANT
Speke's companion on his 1860–1863 expedition was James Grant. Together they made their way to Tabora. Relations with local tribes and Arab traders had soured,

THE SOURCE OF THE NILE

Burton and Speke (1857–1858) ⟶

Speke to Lake Victoria (1858) ⟶

Speke and Grant (1860–1863) ⟶

Baker (1861–1865) ⟶

Above: A map showing attempts to find the source of the Nile. Speke guessed that Lake Victoria was the river's source, but he returned home in 1863 in too much haste to conduct a thorough investigation of the area.

their starting point on the lake shore, reassembled the caravan, and headed back to Tabora. Burton was still suffering terribly from fever and an ulcerated tongue.

On July 10 Speke set out with a small party to investigate reports of another lake to the north. Two weeks later he returned to announce that there was indeed a lake. Speke named it Victoria, in honor of the English queen.

Kennan Ward Photography/Corbis

Above: Lake Tanganyika in Africa's Rift Valley. Where now baboons roam, Burton and Speke stood in February 1858 wondering whether they had found the Nile's source. Burton (right) vehemently championed Tanganyika, but Speke— quite correctly— doubted that it was.

and both treated the white men with suspicion. A first attempt to reach Lake Victoria failed. On their second attempt they skirted around the lake to the west.

Speke then left Grant behind as a hostage with a local chief and found his way to the north side of the lake. In July 1862, after nearly two years in the bush, he came to the point where the Nile flowed out of it, which he named the Ripon Falls. Speke returned to rescue Grant, and the two men made what haste they could downstream to Gondokoro, where they had a rendezvous with an ivory hunter called John Petherick, who was coming up the Nile from the north.

Instead of Petherick they found another explorer, Samuel Baker, who was also looking for the source of the Nile. Speke and Grant then set off down the Nile, leaving Baker and his Hungarian-born wife Florence to continue their explorations in the interior. Speke and Grant returned triumphantly to England.

Their triumph was short lived. They could not prove that Lake Victoria was the Nile's source, nor had they traced the river's course properly between the lake and Gondokoro. The discovery by the Bakers of another lake, Lake Albert, near

Mary Evans Picture Library

Mary Evans Picture Library

This drawing (left) by Captain James Grant, who joined John Speke in 1860, illustrates the hardships of trekking through the African forests.

the warring tribes of the southern Sudan. The British supported the khedive and chose Baker to execute the task.

Baker's expedition was the largest ever mounted in Africa. He sailed up the Nile from Khartoum in a flotilla of 58 boats with 1,600 men on board. But he failed to make the hoped-for breakthrough to Lake Albert, and his military success on behalf of the khedive was wiped out by the 1881–1884 revolt by the Mahdis (Sudanese freedom fighters).

Ric Ergenbright/Corbis

Lake Victoria further complicated matters. Burton continued to press his own claims. A meeting was called to debate the issue in September 1864, presided over by Livingstone. On the day before the meeting Speke died in a shooting accident, and many believed it was suicide.

SAMUEL BAKER

Baker, meanwhile, was still in Africa, exploring the area around Lake Albert. He discovered a spectacular waterfall that he named the Murchison Falls after the then president of the Royal Geographical Society. He did not hear of Speke's death until his return to Khartoum in May 1865. The Nile's source remained a mystery for another 10 years, when the final details were filled in by Henry Stanley and Charles Chaille-Long.

Baker returned to the Nile in 1869. This time his explorations had a political end. His employer, the khedive of Egypt, wanted to establish his authority over

One casualty of the Mahdist revolt was the German-Jewish botanist Eduard Schnitzer. Having converted to Islam, he took the name Emin, to which he added the title Pasha when he became an official in the service of the khedive.

From 1877 Schnitzer explored the area between Lake Albert and the Congo River system. The Mahdist success left Emin Pasha stranded, and in 1887 the American explorer Henry Stanley mounted a relief expedition to rescue him

The spectacular Murchison Falls in Uganda (left) were discovered in 1864 by the British explorer Samuel Baker.

FLORENCE BAKER

Florence von Sass originally came from Transylvania at a time when much of southern Europe was under the rule of the Ottoman Turks. A slight, fair girl, she was spotted in an Ottoman slave market in 1860 by a rich Englishman called Samuel Baker. He bought her and married her, and they set out for Africa together to become explorers.

Florence was a perfect companion for her impulsive husband. In 1862 she rescued him from an angry mob when he was foolishly trying to get his way by force against superior numbers. Two years later it was his turn to rescue her from an attack of malaria so sudden and virulent that she fell "as though shot dead." It did not kill her, and she lived to a ripe old age.

Below: Samuel and Florence Baker riding camels in Africa.

Mary Evans Picture Library

and bring him back to civilization. It is not clear, however, whether Emin wanted to be rescued, least of all by Stanley. He joined the service of the German government and died in the Congo in 1893.

While Samuel Baker and his wife were heading up the Nile, the German explorer Georg Schweinfurth was exploring westward from Khartoum into the Niam-Niam country. Leaving the Nile behind him, he explored the marshes of the

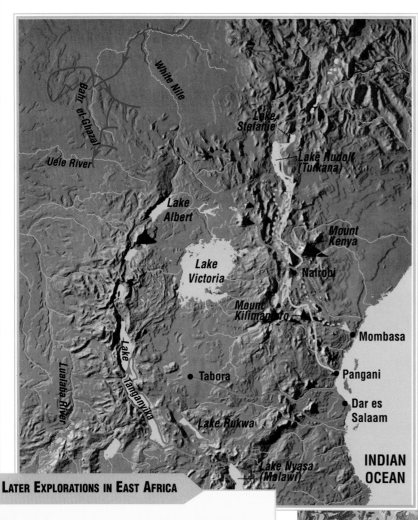

many discoveries, described in detail in his book *The Heart of Africa*. He was also the first European to encounter the pygmies of the Congo forest.

THOMSON'S WINNING WAYS

It was not until 1879 that explorers returned to the area where Rebmann and Krapf had been active in the 1840s. The

Left: A map showing expeditions in East Africa in the late 19th century.

LATER EXPLORATIONS IN EAST AFRICA

Schweinfurth (1869–1871) ⟶

Thomson (1879–1880) ⟶

Thomson (1882–1883)

    outward journey - - - ->

    return journey ⟶

Teleki (1887–1888)

    outward journey ⟶

    return journey - - - ->

Bahr el-Ghazal and came across the Uele River flowing to the west. Wrongly, Schweinfurth supposed that it flowed into the Niger, when in fact the Uele is part of the Congo system. Between the Nile and the Congo, however, he made

AKG, London

50

first to do so was Joseph Thomson, then only 20 years old. Thomson's slogan was "A gentle word is more potent than gunpowder." He was patient and respectful, and no porter ever deserted him. He was ably supported by his caravan-leader Chuma, famous as the devoted companion of David Livingstone 10 years earlier.

In 1879–1880 Thomson steadily proceeded from the coast to the head of Lake Nyasa and on to Lake Tanganyika. From there he made a foray into the Congo before returning to the coast by way of Tabora. The expedition had great scientific value and demonstrated the value of Thomson's humane approach.

Joseph Thomson's slogan was "A gentle word is more potent than gunpowder."

In 1882–1883 Thomson explored the Kenya highlands. He was followed by Harry Johnston, who lacked Thomson's humanity, and by the Hungarian Count Samuel Teleki, who was positively brutal both to the people he met and to his own porters. Teleki's expedition in 1887–1888 did, however, make some important discoveries, including that of Lake Rudolf (now Turkana) in the far north of Kenya.

Teleki was the last of the adventurers in the region. In Tanganyika to the south, Oskar Baumann carried out surveys for the German government, which was laying claims to the territory. Hermann von Wissmann, a former explorer in the Congo, now took over the administration of Tanganyika. For his part Harry Johnston administrated in the areas controlled by the British. The colonial period in East Africa that began in the 1880s lasted until the 1960s.

Left: Eduard "Emin Pasha" Schnitzer hunting Nile crocodiles.

THE ROSETTA STONE

In 1799 a French officer from Napoleon's army in Egypt came across a strange block of black basalt near the town of Rashid, or Rosetta. The stone (below) carried an inscription in Greek and another in two versions of Ancient Egyptian hieroglyphics.

Guessing that the text in both languages was likely to be the same, scholars quickly realized that they had here a clue to the lost Egyptian language and its unique system of writing.

Swedish, British, and French experts puzzled for 20 years over the way the Egyptian hieroglyphics were constructed, with pictures sometimes representing items and at other times standing in for groups of letters. The solution was finally published by the French scholar J.-F. Champollion in 1822.

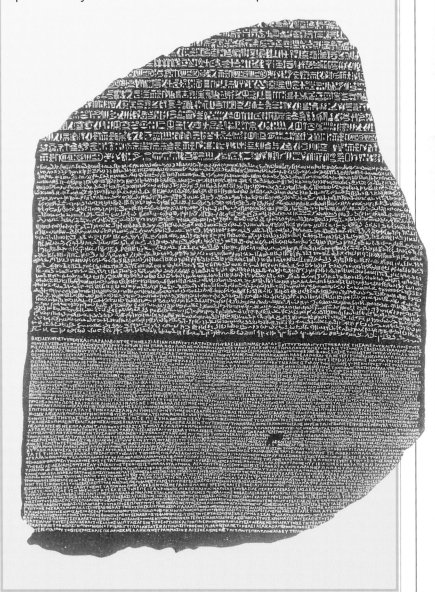

Hulton Getty

WEST AFRICA

When the African Association of Britain was founded in 1788 it was confronted with an extraordinary situation. Three hundred years after the Portuguese had worked their way down the West African coast, the interior remained almost totally unexplored.

Why was this the case? One reason was a sheer lack of interest. European attention was focused on the East and on the Americas. Africa was little more than a staging post on the way to richer prizes elsewhere. European dealings with Africa were minimal. The Portuguese clung to their trading posts, and the Dutch, the English, and the French set up some of their own. But the main trade was in slaves, and so long as slaves were delivered to the coast by native African traders, all that the Europeans needed to do was bring their ships to the coast and carry the human cargo away.

In many parts of Africa European explorers were likely to meet a bullet or a spear (below). Those who trekked up-river faced other dangers, such as man-eating crocodiles (right).

Jonathan Blair/Corbis

AKG, London

Travel in Africa also proved to be difficult and dangerous, particularly on the west coast. The problems were of three kinds: hostile peoples, hazardous terrain, and disease. Many explorers were killed by locals, others were defeated by natural obstacles and forced to turn back, and many more contracted deadly fevers.

Native Africans had every reason to be suspicious of the intruders. Arrogance on the part of the whites, rivalries between tribes, and tensions over the slave trade all contributed to a situation in which it was not easy to distinguish friend from foe.

Travel was made difficult by hostile peoples, rough terrain, and disease.

Organizing expeditions was not easy. Some explorers preferred to travel light, taking only a native guide or interpreter. This way they presented less of a threat to the local peoples, but if they did get into trouble, they were on their own.

As time went on, however, expeditions grew larger and larger. Two or three white men would lead a column of 100 or more African bearers. In each area they passed through they or their interpreter would have to negotiate a right to cross the territory, to buy water and food, and to find a place to set up camp. Supplies needed to be unpacked, mosquito nets set up, changes of clothing brought out. The bearers carried the white men's personal goods, plus cloth and beads to use for barter. Then there was ammunition—which needed to be carefully guarded—and scientific instruments.

DANGEROUS WATERS

The terrain was also difficult. In the absence of roads the obvious way to travel through dense forests was by water, but the West African rivers were not easy to navigate. Some, like the Niger, form marshy deltas near the coast, making it hard to find a clear channel along which to set out upstream.

When explorers did manage to work their way upstream from the coast, they soon found their path blocked by cataracts. The continent of Africa consists mainly of a raised plateau that starts some way inland from the coast, and at some point every African river gushes over impassable waterfalls. The water, too, was dangerous. At any moment hostile local peoples hidden on the banks could unleash poisoned arrows on unsuspecting intruders, or a hippopotamus could capsize a boat and leave the crew at the mercy of crocodiles.

DEADLY BITES

The worst problem facing travelers was disease. All tropical climates are home to many lethal or crippling afflictions, and West Africa was particularly bad. Worst of all was tripanosomiasis, spread by the bite of the tsetse fly. Its symptoms included violent fever and lethargy—hence its more common name of sleeping sickness. The disease also produced a curious craving for meat that sometimes led victims to tear at their own flesh.

Above: Two children suffering from sleeping sickness, one of many diseases that afflicted early explorers.

Hulton Getty/Corbis

Malaria

Malaria is spread by the bite of certain mosquito species and is found all over the world, particularly in marshy tropical regions. In the 19th century the only known treatment for it was quinine, a drug extracted from the bark of a Peruvian tree. But quinine does not destroy malarial infection. Many Europeans died of malaria long after leaving Africa because they mistakenly thought it was safe to stop taking their dose.

Many West Africans, however, are immune to malaria. They carry a genetic mutation known as sickle cell that produces a form of anemia and prevents the malaria parasites spreading through the bloodstream. Some African-Americans also carry this mutation, as do a few white people in Portugal—who may possibly have African blood.

Wild animals were immune to sleeping sickness, but horses, donkeys, and domestic cattle were not. This meant that Arab and European explorers could not use pack animals but had to employ human porters instead. Worse, from the locals' point of view, was the fact that domestic cattle could not be raised for food or for plowing, which meant that the economy remained primitive.

For as long as travel was rare, many diseases were confined to small areas, and the local population acquired some immunity to them. However, the opening up of the world after 1500 meant that diseases were carried to places where they were previously unknown, causing horrendous epidemics. In the 1880s sleeping sickness spread to Central and East Africa and destroyed whole communities. Conversely, relapsing fever, which

Mary Evans Picture Library

Left: Scottish surgeon Mungo Park. The London-based African Association sent Park out in 1795 to study the Niger River.

The story of the discovery of the Niger River illustrates the sort of dangers faced by early explorers. Almost all of them met an early death—killed by tribesmen, stricken by disease, or victims of physical conditions. Indeed, the Niger basin came to be known to Europeans as the White Man's Grave.

was originally limited to East Africa, spread across the continent to affect West Africa as well.

Other dangerous diseases included malaria and dysentery, which affected Europeans far more seriously than they did Africans. Yellow fever also entered Africa, probably from South America.

Below: Routes taken by European explorers in West Africa, including investigations of the Niger River.

WEST AFRICAN EXPLORATION

Houghton (1790–1791) ———————▶

● Death of Houghton

Mungo Park (1795–1797) ———————▶

Mungo Park (1805–1806) – – – – ▶

● Death of Park

Clapperton and Lander (1825–1827) ———————▶

Caillié (1827–1828) ———————▶

Lander brothers (1830) ———————▶

Binger (1887–1889) ———————▶

SAHARA

Timbuktu

Niger River

Djenné

Segou

Gambia River

Bamako

Niger River

Sokoto

Kano

Ougadougou

Black Volta

White Volta

BENIN

Bussa Rapids

Kong

Komoe River

Niger River

ATLANTIC OCEAN

Badagry

Niger Delta

The first explorer sent to West Africa by the African Association in 1790 was Major Daniel Houghton. He made a good start up the Gambia valley and found his way into the upper Niger basin, but was robbed and killed by local tribesmen.

The Association then turned to a young man recommended by the wealthy botanist Sir Joseph Banks, one of its founder members and a former member of Captain James Cook's round-the-world expedition in 1768–1771. Banks's choice was a Scottish surgeon, then barely 24 years old, called Mungo Park.

Park set out from England in May 1795. He brought with him no equipment other than a compass, a thermometer, a sextant, and a couple of pistols. He did not speak Arabic, though he did take the trouble on arriving in Africa to learn the Mandingo language of local traders.

THE MAJESTIC NIGER

In December 1795, taking a similar route to Houghton's, Park crossed into the Niger basin—only to be captured by a local Muslim ruler who threatened to kill him. Park was finally released, and in July 1796 he reached the objective of his mission: "the majestic Niger, glittering to the morning sun…and flowing slowly *to the eastward*." He had solved part of the

Below: The village of Kamalia, where Mungo Park spent seven months ill with a fever. When he finally managed to make his way back to the mouth of the Gambia River, he found everyone had given him up for dead.

Mary Evans Picture Library

THE SLAVE TRADE

The European trade in African slaves began in the 16th century. It was a so-called triangular trade. European manufactured goods were sold to Arab and African traders in exchange for slaves; the slaves were transported to the Americas to work on the plantations in North America, the Caribbean, and Brazil. Sugar, tobacco, and other products from the plantations were shipped back to Europe. These imports were competitively priced—because the labor was cheap.

It was also a brutal trade. Eleven million Africans were shipped to America, and maybe a million died in transit. Survivors could be subjected to any treatment their masters wished. Attempts to abolish slavery grew in force, and by the time of the Civil War of 1861–1865 only Brazil was receiving slaves from Africa.

Below: Slaves embarking for the West. Many would have been rounded up by local African and Arab traders.

Mary Evans Picture Library

mystery of the the Niger, but he was also very sick. Friendly traders nursed him back to health and then took him back to Gambia, where he arrived in June 1797.

In 1805 Park returned to Africa, this time as the leader of a large expedition. Park and his companions left their base in Gambia in May and reached the Niger valley just before the rainy season. The heat was unbearable, and the rains, when they came, brought fever.

By the time Park reached the Niger in August, all his pack animals had died and so had two-thirds of the European members of the party. Park himself was feverish. The survivors launched a boat and sailed downriver. They passed Timbuktu and continued southeast into the Hausa country. There were now only four men left. Reaching the Bussa rapids, they were attacked by locals. Nobody knows quite what happened; Park and his companions may have been killed by their attackers, or they may have been drowned in the rapids. None survived.

Park had proved that the Niger River flowed east along the southern edge of the Sahara and then turned south toward the Gulf of Guinea. He had also shown that an explorer in Africa needed to be strong, resourceful—and young.

The mystery of the Niger was still not entirely solved. In the early 1820s expeditions were sent out both southward across the Sahara and inland from the West African coast to find out more about it. One man, Hugh Clapperton, was involved in both approaches. With Denham and Oudney he had crossed the Sahara to Lake Chad in 1823–1824. Then in 1825, with Richard Lander and a few other companions, he set out from the Benin coast into the interior.

Nik Wheeler/Corbis

Mary Evans Picture Library

Above: Wearing outsize sunhats, Richard and John Lander meet the king of Badagry at the start of their 1830 trek to the Niger River (right).

Within weeks the whole party was struck down by fever. Only Clapperton, Lander, and their Hausa guide survived. The three crossed the Niger at Bussa, where Park had died, and eventually reached Sokoto. Here Clapperton fell ill with dysentery and died. Lander struggled back to the coast on his own.

Despite the horrors he had witnessed on his trip, Lander made a second journey to Africa in 1830, this time with his brother John. The brothers reached the Niger at Bussa and, after some tense negotiation with warring local chiefs, set sail downstream. On the way they were captured and had to be ransomed but they finally found their way to the Niger Delta and out to sea.

Weakened by scurvy, Caillié set out from Timbuktu to cross the Sahara Desert.

Meanwhile the French Geographical Society had offered a prize of 10,000 francs for the first man to reach the fabled city of Timbuktu and bring back a report. A young French explorer, René-August Caillié, determined to win it.

To TIMBUKTU AND BACK

Caillié was the son of a village baker in rural France and had run away to sea as a cabin boy when he was 17. He fetched up on the West African coast where he jumped ship and joined a British expedition in search of Mungo Park.

He later returned to France for seven years and then spent time in the British colony of Sierra Leone superintending a plantation. When he heard of the prize, he returned to Africa. He decided to travel alone, disguised as a Muslim.

Caillié's strategy proved a good one. Starting out from the Guinea coast in March 1827, he attached himself to Arab

Christel Gerstenberg/Corbis

Above: Tuareg nomads of northern Africa. When René Caillié reached Timbuktu in 1828, Muslim traders told him how the Tuareg had tortured and murdered the British explorer Major Alexander Laing who had reached the city three years earlier.

caravans and succeeded in reaching Timbuktu, where he spent two weeks. From there he headed across the desert to Tangier and eventually returned to Paris. He was awarded the prize—although some people doubted whether he had really been to Timbuktu, as his description of the city did not match the popular idea of it.

The British largely lost interest in the Niger. In 1854 William Baikie, coming up from the coast, attempted to link up with Heinrich Barth in the area of Lake Chad. He did not find Barth but did sail up the Benue for 300 miles (480 km) and confirmed Barth's observations of it. Richard Burton also spent time in West Africa. But for most of the rest of the century the exploration of West Africa belonged to the French and the Germans.

FRENCH AND GERMAN EXPLOITS

Germany now had designs on West Africa, and the German African Society sent out many explorers in the 1870s and 1880s. The new generation of German explorers combined scientific interests with a mission to claim territory on behalf of their government.

The French explorer Louis-Gustav Binger also belonged to this new generation. In 1887–1889 he thoroughly surveyed the area between the Niger valley and that of the Black Volta River. In so doing he demolished many fanciful notions about the geography of the area.

GOVERNOR OF THE IVORY COAST

In 1892 Binger did equally valuable work on the boundary between the British Gold Coast and the French Ivory Coast, partly with a view to establishing a formal frontier between what were now two colonies. In recognition of his skills he was appointed governor of the Ivory Coast in 1893.

Below: While exploring between the Niger and Volta rivers, Louis-Gustav Binger discovered the ancient town of Bikasso.

Kevin Schafer/Corbis

e.t.archive

Left, Vol

Left: Tree roots in the tropical rainforests of Cameroon. Richard Burton hacked through these dense jungles in 1861, while serving as a diplomat in the Gulf of Guinea.

Below: The philanthropist and explorer Mary Kingsley traveling the Ogowe River in stately style.

The Englishwoman Mary Kingsley also represented a new generation of explorers. Brought up in a progressive family, she devoted her early life to looking after her parents. When they died, she seized the opportunity to put her scientific interests to the test in the most adventurous way possible.

"FISH AND FETISH"

In 1893 Kingsley embarked for West Africa to study its wildlife and its people or, as she put it, "fish and fetish." Her travels took her all over West Africa as far south as Angola. She sailed in canoes, tramped through the forests, and ascended the 12,000-foot (3,600-m) Great Peak of the Cameroons. On her return to England she became a campaigner against what she saw as an inhumane system of colonial administration.

By the end of the 19th century West Africa counted as fully explored, although much remained poorly mapped.

Mary Evans Picture Library

Into the Interior

The last parts of Africa to be explored were the forests and uplands of equatorial Central Africa. Portuguese explorers had gone some way up the Congo but had hesitated to go far into forests, where it was said that cannibals lurked.

The Portuguese also considered an approach to the interior from the eastern side, up the Zambezi, where they had outposts. In 1797 Francisco de Lacerda made his way inland and came close to discovering Lake Nyasa. But the benefits of exploring far were not clear, and for a long time caution prevailed over the spirit of adventure.

Exploration was entering the industrial age, bringing remote frontiers ever closer.

Technology came to the explorers' aid. In the mid-19th century steam began to replace sail on ships. This in itself made the long outward voyage easier, but shipbuilders had yet another trick up their sleeves. A powerful steamer could sail from Europe and into the lower reaches of the Congo or Zambezi. There it would disgorge parts of a smaller ship that could be carried up past rapids and assembled higher up. Exploration was entering the industrial age, which brought the remote frontiers ever closer.

Even with technology to help them, however, explorers still found Central Africa fraught with dangers and difficulties, and they had to be brave, resourceful, and often cunning.

One man who had these qualities in abundance was Dr. David Livingstone. In 1853 Livingstone was given permission by the London Missionary Society to return to the Makalolo people, near the Zambezi, whom he had first visited two years earlier. During 10 years in South Africa Livingstone had made few converts, but he had proved himself as an explorer. He managed to persuade the society that the king of the Makalolo was well disposed to the Christian religion and to European settlement.

When Livingstone reached Makalolo territory, he found that his old friend King Sebituane was dead. But the new king, 18-year-old Sekeletu, was friendly. When Livingstone decided to head west toward the Congo, Sekeletu lent him a team of hand-picked warriors to accompany him.

Livingstone crosses Africa

In November 1853 Livingstone and his party set off from Sesheke up the Zambezi, crossed to the Congo basin, and made their way cross-country to the coast at Luanda. After resting for three months to recover from the effects of dysentery and malaria, Livingstone set out on the return trek in September 1854.

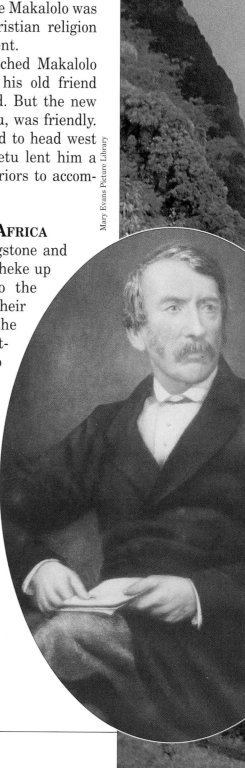

Stephen Frink/Corbis

Mary Evans Picture Library

Right: The Scottish missionary Dr. David Livingstone first went to Africa in 1840 and soon gained experience with exploration. It was in 1855 that he came across the breathtaking Victoria Falls (right) on the Zambezi River.

Mary Evans Picture Library

Left: The Ma Robert, Livingstone's steam launch, navigating the Zambezi River in 1858.

During the late 1850s Livingstone made a series of trips up the Shire River (below). In 1859 he came across Lake Nyasa.

It took him nearly a year to return to Sekeletu's base near the Zambezi. There he paused again before embarking on the final leg of his journey. He reached the Zambezi, and on November 17, 1855, he came to a point where the river, over a mile (1.6 km) wide, tumbles several hundred feet down a spectacular waterfall. Naming this the Victoria Falls in honor of the British queen, Livingstone pushed on down the valley to Tete and from there to the coast at Quelimane.

Livingstone had crossed the continent from west to east. He may not have been the first European ever to do this, but he was certainly the first to do so with the world's eyes focused on him.

EXPLORING BY RIVER BOAT

Although he was now a popular hero, Livingstone had still made no converts, and the London Missionary Society grew tired of waiting. The British government stepped in and appointed him consul for the Zambezi, putting a small steam launch at his disposal to assist his journeys up the river.

In the summer of 1858 Livingstone sailed up the Zambezi to Tete, hoping to continue to Victoria Falls. However, his passage was blocked by a waterfall as tall as a tree at the Quebrabasa Gorge near Tete, and he had to turn back. Undaunted, he then sailed up the Shire River, only to discover that it too was blocked by cataracts.

ANOTHER GREAT LAKE

In 1859 Livingstone made further trips up the Shire, taking his launch as far as it could go and then proceeding on foot. In September he discovered Lake Nyasa, second only to Lake Tanganyika in length. The discoveries he was making were of more than local importance for African geography. They provided Sir Roderick Murchison, president of Britain's Royal Geographical Society, with confirmation for his general theory about the structure of the continent.

Livingstone was sometimes a difficult man and quarreled with members of his expeditions, particularly with the artist Thomas Baines. Such quarrels among

Hulton Getty

explorers were quite common, particularly under the effects of fever, and were usually patched up quickly. But this dispute with Baines was not resolved. Baines, who produced the most beautiful paintings of the Zambezi landscape, was unjustly dismissed by Livingstone, and the two men were never reconciled.

INTO THE HEART OF AFRICA

In 1864 Livingstone returned to England, but in 1866 he was back in Africa. His journey would take him deep into the heart of Central Africa in search of the source of the Nile River. It also forced him into an unwelcome alliance. He was a staunch opponent of the slave

SIDI BOMBAY

Sidi Mubarak, known as Sidi Bombay, was caravan leader for many African explorations. Born into the East African Yao tribe, at the age of 12 he was captured by bandits and sold into slavery. His Arab master took him to Bombay in India, which is how he got his nickname. As chief interpreter for Richard Burton and John Speke on their 1857 search for the sources of the Nile, he earned a medal from the British Royal Geographical Society for his diplomatic skills.

Sidi accompanied Henry Stanley to his famous meeting with Dr. David Livingstone in 1871 but could not take Stanley's bullying and went to work for Verney Cameron instead. He then retired, dying in 1886 a respected figure in his community.

trade, but the areas he was now exploring were dominated by Arab slave traders. The doctor was obliged to seek protection from the most fearsome trader of all, an Arab known as Tippu Tip.

The early stages of the journey were promising. Livingstone discovered lakes Mweru and Bangweulu to the west of Lake Nyasa and then made his way north to Ujiji on Lake Tanganyika.

Then everything started to go wrong. His porters deserted. Supplies requested from Zanzibar failed to arrive. He spent much of 1870 racked with fever.

> *The doctor was obliged to seek protection from the fearsome trader Tippu Tip.*

At the beginning of the following year Livingstone decided on a last-ditch effort to trace the source of the Nile. Crossing to the west side of the lake, he went in search of the Lualaba River, which he thought might be one of the sources of the Nile. On his way back to Ujiji he was ambushed by tribesmen and was lucky to escape with his life. He was now at his wits' end. He did not know if any of the urgent messages he had sent back to Zanzibar had got through. He had no supplies and no money.

LIVINGSTONE IS MISSING!

Unknown to Livingstone, his plight had now become a worldwide concern. In October 1869 the powerful American newspaper editor James Bennett Jr. summoned one of his crack reporters and presented him with a two-word assignment: "Find Livingstone!"

This crack reporter was a young man called Henry Morton Stanley. Born in Wales, he had gone to sea as a boy and jumped ship in New Orleans. He then served on both sides in the American

Below: The expedition routes of David Livingstone, Henry Stanley, and Verney Cameron in Central Africa. Livingstone and Stanley both crossed Africa, exhibiting very different styles of leadership.

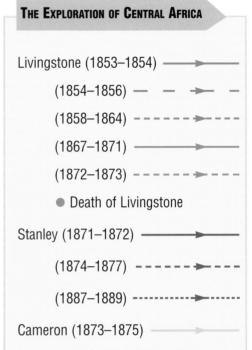

THE EXPLORATION OF CENTRAL AFRICA

Livingstone (1853–1854)	———▶
(1854–1856)	— — ▶ —
(1858–1864)	-----▶
(1867–1871)	———▶
(1872–1873)	-----▶
● Death of Livingstone	
Stanley (1871–1872)	———▶
(1874–1877)	- - - -▶ -
(1887–1889)	·······▶
Cameron (1873–1875)	———▶

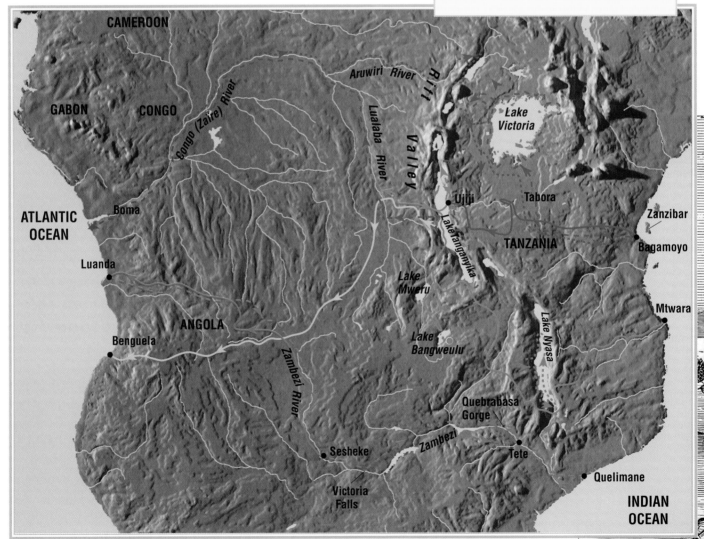

AKG, London

Library of Congress/Corbis

Left: Stanley crossing a swamp in search of Livingstone in 1871. On finding the sick doctor stranded at Ujiji (above) the newspaperman uttered the immortal greeting, "Doctor Livingstone, I presume?"

Civil War before choosing journalism. He had already had one scoop in Africa before Bennett chose him for his new task.

With the vast resources of the *New York Herald* behind him, Stanley set out from Zanzibar early in 1871 at the head of a party of 200. The Nyamwezi tribe were rebelling against the Arabs, and Stanley had to take evasive action. He reached Ujiji at the end of October 1871. Having been informed that a white man had arrived in the town, Livingstone left his hut and went to meet the newcomer.

"Dr. Livingstone, I presume?" said the American. "I thank God I have been permitted to shake hands with you."

success at finding the doctor. Meanwhile, Livingstone made his way back to Lake Bangweulu. Finally the accumulated effects of all his illnesses caught up with him, and he died there on May 1, 1873.

VERNEY CAMERON

With the doctor when he died were his two black head porters, Susi and Chuma. They embalmed his body with salt and alcohol and set off with it toward the coast. On the way they met another Scottish explorer, Verney Cameron, who was searching for Livingstone. While Susi and Chuma continued on their journey, Cameron decided that he should continue Livingstone's work.

"I feel thankful that I am here to welcome you," replied the doctor.

Livingstone and Stanley immediately struck up a friendship. They traveled together to the northern end of Lake Tanganyika, where they established that the Rusizi flows into the lake rather than out of it and therefore could not be part of the Nile. Stanley now proposed taking Livingstone back to the coast, but the doctor refused: he still felt he had work to do in finding the sources of the Nile. Stanley made his way to Zanzibar and returned to England, triumphant in his

Livingstone was in a pitiful state during his last days and had to be carried by his porters (above). "I am excessively weak," he wrote on April 20, 1873. Eleven days later he died.

Mary Evans Picture Library

Below: Verney Cameron on his journey to the west coast in 1875. Cameron had been sent out in 1872 to find David Livingstone; on hearing that the doctor had died, Cameron stayed on to explore.

Accompanied by the loyal interpreter Sidi Bombay, Cameron first completed an extensive survey of the southern end of Lake Tanganyika. He then set out in David Livingstone's footsteps to the Lualaba River, which he reached in August 1874.

With help from the trader Tippu Tip, Cameron now struck westward into Katanga. Finally, in November of the following year he emerged at Benguela on the Atlantic coast, having crossed the continent from east to west.

THE IVORY TRADE

Ivory, the hard dentine forming the tusk of an elephant, has been in demand for its creamy color and fine texture since ancient times. Skilled craftsmen from civilizations throughout the world have produced exquisitive carvings from the material. The trade slumped after the 19th century when elephant numbers were decimated by hunters and traders.

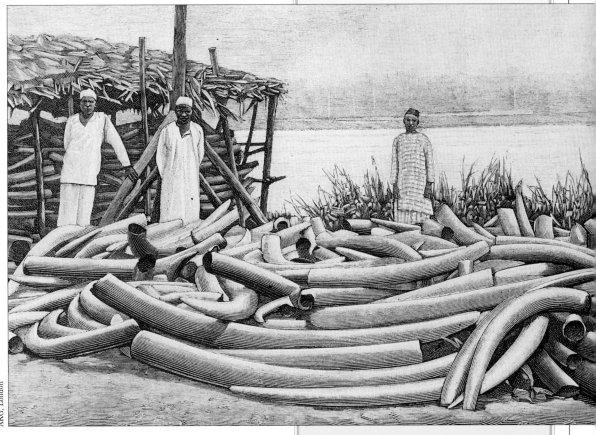

AKG, London

Above: Some of the ivory stockpiled at the Stanley Falls by the Arab trader Tippu Tip during the 1880s.

Stanley, meanwhile, had plans of his own. In November 1874 he led a huge expedition inland from Bagamoyo on the east coast. He was a harsh taskmaster, and many porters died on the journey, but he simply hired more to replace those lost to disease, desertion, or fighting.

In 1875 the expedition explored the shores of Lake Victoria, and in 1876 it explored Lake Tanganyika. Stanley then trekked to the Lualaba River and followed it to the point where it becomes the Congo, and then all the way downstream to the coast. He reached Boma on the Atlantic coast on August 9, 1877, so com-

Mary Evans Picture Library

Missionaries like Livingstone believed that trade would benefit the Africans as well as the Europeans. In order to trade, the Europeans began to carve out zones of influence, with the British particularly active on the east coast and the French increasingly on the west.

In 1879 King Leopold of Belgium decided to establish a personal empire for himself in the Congo. To this end he employed none other than Henry Stanley, who by this time was bored with journalism. Between 1879 and 1884 Stanley set up trading stations all the way up the Congo, putting down local resistance by force of arms. Then, in 1887 he headed up the Congo valley and crossed to the Rift Valley, where he made the European discovery of the Ruwenzori Mountains.

THE SCRAMBLE FOR AFRICA

A typical figure of the late 19th century was Hermann von Wissmann, a German army officer who went to Africa in 1880. Wissmann cooperated with Belgian and German explorers in the Congo but then

pleting the east–west crossing of the continent two years after Cameron had done so. His journey had taken him 999 days.

FRENCH AND PORTUGUESE INROADS

Meanwhile, on the west coast French, German, and Portuguese explorers were making inroads. Paul du Chaillu, the son of a French merchant in Gabon, explored the rainforest in the 1850s. A collector of stuffed animals, he had the dubious distinction of being the first European to shoot a gorilla. In 1875–1877 Pierre de Brazza explored the Ogowe River.

In Angola, where the Portuguese were settled, German scientists carried out many detailed surveys. But the successes of Cameron and Stanley had alerted the Portuguese to the strategic importance of exploration. They sent Major Aleixandre Serpa Pinto on a transcontinental expedition from Benguela to Natal in 1877.

CARVING UP THE CONTINENT

By now exploration was a pawn in the political games of the European powers. From the beginning trade had been a major objective of the European associations that sent explorers out to Africa.

Henry Stanley led enormous expeditions (above) and named several places after himself.

Brian Vikander/Corbis

Right: Hermann von Wissmann (seated on the left) was one of a new breed of explorers—civil servants and military men helping their country stake a claim in a piece of Africa. Wissmann's main aim was to bring a large part of eastern central Africa under German administration. This included the rolling savannas of Tanganyika (modern-day Tanzania, below).

AKG, London

in 1888 led a march across the continent to Lakes Tanganyika and Nyasa and out to the sea at Quelimane. From then on he worked for the German government in East Africa, helping to turn Tanganyika (now Tanzania) into a German colony.

George Grenfell, a Protestant missionary, spent nearly 30 years in the Congo basin, mapping its many rivers and trying to keep aloof from politics. In 1902 Grenfell published his map of the Congo River system, based on his own researches and those of Belgian and German explorers. Some rivers appeared as dotted lines, but the map was remarkably complete. On every disputed frontier surveyors were mapping the features that could mark borders between the new colonies. Administrators and surveyors took over from explorers. Yet even today, Central Africa still has secrets to yield up.

SET INDEX

Numbers in **bold type** are volume numbers.

Page numbers in *italics* refer to picture captions or a caption and text reference on the same page.

VIRGINIA

NORWALK PUBLIC LIBRARY

3 1294 06160 6796

R
J910.9   The Grolier student
Gro   library of explorers
V.8   and exploration.

SO. NORWALK BRANCH LIBRARY
10 Washington Street
Norwalk, CT 06854
Tel. 899-2790

FOR REFERENCE

Do Not Take From This Room